Nearly every book about Rhode Island has to explain itself before it addresses its subject at hand. How can anything dealing with something as small as Rhode Island matter in the wider scheme of things? Dr. Patrick T. Conley's work portraying the founders of Rhode Island answers the question once and for all. This assembly of persons was truly extraordinary, not only in launching a great lively experiment in civil self-government in the towns around Narragansett Bay, but also for the ideas and precedents they set for the American nation. Conley's eye for pertinent detail and also his gaze for the greater picture of American history has once again captured the micro and the macro of history in an engaging and enlightening way.

—Albert T. Klyberg, LHD

Rhode Island's FOUNDERS

FROM SETTLEMENT TO STATEHOOD

PATRICK T. CONLEY

PHOTOGRAPHY BY TERACE GREENE

THE
History
PRESS

Published by The History Press
Charleston, SC 29403
www.historypress.net

Copyright © 2010 by Patrick T. Conley and the
Rhode Island Heritage Hall of Fame

First published 2010
Second printing 2011
Third printing 2012

ISBN 9781540220301

Library of Congress Cataloging-in-Publication Data

Conley, Patrick T.
Rhode Island's founders : from settlement to statehood / Patrick T. Conley.
p. cm.
Includes bibliographical references.

1. Rhode Island--Biography. 2. Rhode Island--History--Colonial period, ca.
1600-1775--Biography. 3. Rhode Island--History--1775-1865--Biography. 4. Pioneers-
-Rhode Island--Biography. 5. Clergy--Rhode Island--Biography. 6. Revolutionaries--
Rhode Island--Biography. 7. Politicians--Rhode Island--Biography. 8. Soldiers--Rhode
Island--Biography. I. Title.
F78.C66 2010
974.5'01--dc22
2010004954

This book is dedicated to

Julia V. (Maney) Conley
(1908–2010)

*who died just as this volume went to press, less than two weeks prior
to her 102nd birthday. Julia was a beloved aunt who helped to raise
me; an amateur historian who enriched my knowledge of local history
with her reminiscences; and our family's published genealogist, who
uncovered the Conley roots in Ireland and America.*

Contents

CONTENTS

$$\mathscr{Preface}$$

In March 1965, a small group of Rhode Island civic leaders, led by sports journalist and cartoonist Frank Lanning, created the Rhode Island Heritage Hall of Fame. The hall was founded "to honor the contributions of those whose efforts, in any line of endeavor, have added significantly to the heritage of the State of Rhode Island." These founders stated that "eligible membership may include those who are native-born, those whose reputations have been made while residents of the state, and those who have adopted Rhode Island as their permanent home." The early citations for such inductees concluded with the phrase "for your contributions to your community, state, and nation," suggesting that mere fame without at least a preponderance of virtue would not merit selection.

Accordingly, there are some omissions in the hall's roster of "founders" that would demand space in a neutral dictionary of Rhode Island biography. The most conspicuous of those considered for election, but rejected, was the influential and multidimensional John Brown, denied because of his persistent advocacy of the slave trade in the face of efforts to abolish it. The same stigma applies to John's much less versatile brother Nicholas (1729–1791), a highly successful Providence merchant, and to Aaron Lopez, Newport's Jewish American merchant prince, who was heavily involved in what he termed "the Guinea traffic." Also omitted from the Hall of Fame was the illustrious and industrious Jemima Wilkinson (1752–1819) of Cumberland, a religious charlatan who styled herself as the "Public Universal Friend" and claimed to be the second coming of Jesus Christ, as well as artist Gilbert

Stuart (1755–1828), whose heyday was the Early National Period and not the span covered in this volume.

The reader will note that the fifty-six biographical profiles included in these pages, like encyclopedia entries, are uneven in length. This disparity, most notable in the treatment given Roger Williams, is due mainly to the desire to give space to Hall of Fame inductees in proportion to their influence on Rhode Island or the nation—or, in the case of Williams, the world. Accordingly, figures such as Anne Hutchinson, Stephen Hopkins, Nathanael Greene, James Mitchell Varnum and Robert Gray receive fuller profiles than purely local personalities. Other factors affecting length of treatment might include the multidimensional nature of the subject, the length of his or her productive career, the duration of time spent in Rhode Island or, simply, the amount of information available on his or her life. It will also be seen that the profiles are arranged and presented in rough chronology.

In the Hall of Fame's early years, its board focused on contemporary Rhode Islanders, especially athletes. Therefore, only eight of the fifty-six founders profiled herein had been selected prior to 1997. In 1972, as a young history professor, I had written to the board to suggest (using the baseball analogy) that it create an "old-timers committee," composed of state historians, to recognize and induct significant early Rhode Islanders. My letter received no reply, presumably because board members felt sure that they had rounded up what detectives call "the usual suspects": Roger Williams, Stephen Hopkins, Nathanael Greene and a handful of others.

In 1995, I was chosen for induction, primarily (I am told) because of my writings in the field of Rhode Island history. The year following, the Hall of Fame's then-president, Manny Gorriaran Jr., invited me to become a board member, an honor I readily accepted. This appointment, plus my status as inductee, gave me the opportunity to renew my 1972 suggestion for a Historians' Committee. How could Pat Conley be a Hall of Famer, I asked, when people such as Massasoit, Anne Hutchinson, Dr. John Clarke, King Philip and General James Mitchell Varnum, among others, were not? President Gorriaran agreed and supported the establishment of my long-awaited Historians' Committee, consisting at various times of Al Klyberg, Paul Campbell, Scott Molloy, Glenn Laxton, James Marusak and Fred Williamson. In various ways, they have all contributed to this volume, especially Al Klyberg, who wrote the original versions of several profiles.

When I suggested this kind of book to The History Press in response to its initiative, the editors, particularly Saunders Robinson, asked several pointed questions, the chief of which was this: in view of the fact that the hall has inducted over 640 members to date, where would the book end? Giovanni da Verrazzano was the obvious starting point (notwithstanding the prior claims advanced for the Vikings, Miguel Corte-Real and others), and soon the elusive terminal date (or decades) became increasingly obvious to me. As the chairman of Rhode Island's bicentennial of statehood celebration in May 1990, I found it natural to select the achievement of statehood as the concluding event for this volume—a book about Rhode Island, from colony to state.

Included here are biographical profiles of fifty-six men and women whose efforts led to the creation of a prosperous, diverse, innovative and independent state within the American union—the restless and turbulent PIONEERS; the cultured early eighteenth-century STABILIZERS; and the bold REVOLUTIONARIES. Wherever possible, the illustrations are likenesses of the subject, although some of these are posthumous artistic recreations. Where no likeness exists, an object associated with the person has been used, such as a signature, book or monument.

The inclusion of these "founders" in the Rhode Island Hall of Fame not only gives that pantheon of eminent Rhode Islanders a comprehensiveness and legitimacy that it once lacked, but it also provides present-day Rhode Islanders with illustrious models to admire and, hopefully, to emulate.

Acknowledgements

All books are cooperative projects. This one is no different. My collaborators were the board of directors of the Rhode Island Heritage Hall of Fame, which provided generous financial assistance; board member Al Klyberg, who read the manuscript and offered valuable suggestions for its contents; Terace Greene, who supplied all of the volume's photographic material, including photos of her own creation; Hilliard Beller, who improved the book's style with his meticulous copyediting; Anna Loiselle and Linda Gallen, my dedicated and able legal secretaries, who have repeatedly doubled as book typists; my daughter, Colleen Conley, who diligently served as my search engine, mining the Internet for valuable information on our founders not readily available elsewhere; and finally, my wife, Gail, who cheerfully suffered through yet another disrupting book project while listening and offering suggestions to make this book more palatable to the general reader.

PART I

The Pioneers

Pre-1700

GIOVANNI DA VERRAZZANO

Giovanni da Verrazzano (1485–1528) was an Italian explorer and navigator who sailed in the service of France. Although the exact place and date of his birth have not been positively established, he was probably a native of the Chianti region of Tuscany, well born and well educated. As a young man, he took up residence in Dieppe on France's Normandy coast, from which he made many voyages to the eastern Mediterranean. Having earned a reputation as an excellent sea captain, he entered the service of King Francis I to undertake a voyage to the New World in hope of finding a sea route through the Americas to the Pacific and the Orient. It was the first such expedition to North America under the auspices of the French crown. Accompanied by his younger brother Girolamo, a mapmaker, and a crew of fifty men, Verrazzano crossed the Atlantic in the caravel *La Dauphine* and made landfall at or near Cape Fear, North Carolina, in 1524. After a short voyage southward, he turned toward the north and explored the North American coast, probably as far as Newfoundland, anchoring briefly in the Narrows of New York Harbor and in Narrangansett Bay, where bridges now recall his visit. Although this voyage failed in its primary objective of discovering a passage to China, Verrazzano's report of this expedition, written for Francis I immediately after returning to France, does provide the first geographical description of a large section of the North American

Giovanni da Verrazzano, an Italian navigator sailing in the employ of France, was the first European explorer to record his visit to Rhode Island. This is a modern copy of a posthumous sixteenth-century portrait that was painted by Edward R. Hines and donated to the Rhode Island Heritage Hall of Fame by Robert Hines.

coast based on a known exploration. The land discovered in this voyage was named "Francesca" in honor of the French king. Verrazzano's narrative also contains important data concerning the physical appearance, customs and way of life of the Indian tribes observed during the voyage

Of the early explorers in North America, Verrazzano was the first to name newly found places in honor of prominent personalities or important spots in Europe. With the notable exception of Rhode Island, however, few of these place names have survived. Verrazzano called Block Island "Luisa" in honor of the queen mother of France and likened the "well-peopled" island to the Mediterranean Isle of Rhodes. After anchoring in present-day Newport Harbor, he spent fifteen days exploring the entire Narragansett Bay region as far north as Pawtucket Falls. Displaying a sense of humor, Verrazzano allegedly named the Dumpling Rocks off Jamestown "Petra Viva" for Marie Catherine de Pierre-Vive, the voluptuous wife of a banker who had helped fund his expedition. He called the bay "Refugio."

Verrazzano reported to his royal sponsor that he had observed fertile open fields, forests of oak and cypress, "many kinds of fruit," an "enormous number of animals—stags, deer, lynx, and other species"—and friendly natives. The Italian described the Indians (probably Wampanoags) glowingly:

> *There people are the most beautiful and have the most civil customs that we have found on this voyage. They are taller than we are; they are a bronze color, some tending more toward whiteness, others to a tawny color; the face is clear-cut; the hair is long and black, and they take great pains to decorate it; the eyes are black and alert, and their manner is sweet and gentle.*

Verrazzano's detailed report of his 1524 voyage was read (in translation) by one or more of Rhode Island's first settlers, who misinterpreted it. In 1614, Dutch navigator Adrien Block renamed "Luisa" for himself, contributing to the mix-up whereby the "Rhodes" allusion was affixed to the island of Aquidneck. A 1637 letter from Williams was signed "at Aquednetick [Aquidneck] now called by us Rhode Island." The royal charter of 1663 decreed that the new colony, consisting of two island settlements (Portsmouth and Newport) and the mainland "plantations" of Providence and Warwick, be named "Rhode Island and Providence Plantations." Thus, by indirection and misinterpretation, Verrazzano gave the state its name. In a subsequent expedition in 1527, sponsored in part by French admiral Philippe de Chabot, Verrazzano reached the Brazilian coast, from which he brought back a valuable cargo of logwood to France. Verrazzano's third voyage, which got underway in the spring of 1528, ended in tragedy for the captain. The great navigator attempted on that occasion to find a passage to Asia south of the area that he had explored in the first voyage. Apparently, he followed the chain of the Lesser Antilles and stopped at one of the islands, possibly Guadeloupe, where hostile Caribs seized, killed and then ate him. His 1524 experience with the hospitable Wampanoags perhaps influenced him to become easy prey.

CHIEF SACHEM MASSASOIT (OUSAMEQUIN)

The Wampanoags historically were a tribe of horticulturists, farmers, fishermen and woodland hunters who inhabited eastern Rhode Island and southeastern Massachusetts. Their name means "People of the East" or "People of the Dawn." Their tribal organization was in the nature of a confederacy of small bands. These varied sub-tribes, with their approximate areas of settlement, included: the Aquinnah (Martha's Vineyard); the Mashpee, Nauset and Manomet (Cape Cod); the Seakonke (the Blackstone Valley from East Providence to Cumberland); the Pawtuxet (the area of present-day Plymouth); the Troy (Fall River); the Assonet (the town of Assonet northward to Taunton); the Herring Pond (near Wareham); the Nemasket (Middleboro and environs); the Pocasset (Tiverton and Portsmouth); the Sakonnet or Sogkonate (Little Compton); and the Pokanoket (present-day Bristol County, Rhode Island).

In 1616–17, the Wampanoags were victimized by a severe smallpox epidemic (a disease introduced by Europeans for which the natives had no built-in immunity). The Pawtuxet, in particular, were devastated, leaving their area around Plymouth open to settlement by the Pilgrims and weakening the power of Massasoit, a Pokanoket and the reigning chief sachem of the Wampanoag confederation.

Massasoit, also known as Ousamequin (ca. 1581–1661), was born in present-day Rhode Island, probably in Bristol, but little is known of his parents or his early life. As chief sachem of the Wampanoag nation, which stretched from Narragansett Bay through Cape Cod and its islands and as far north as Middleboro and Plymouth, he befriended the Pilgrims, taught them farming methods and joined with them in a legendary thanksgiving feast in 1621. Massasoit attended that three-day celebration in late autumn with approximately ninety Wampanoags and supplied the gathering with five deer and other food.

Massasoit was aided in his relations with Plymouth by Squanto and Samoset, two natives who had learned the English language as a result of their abduction by traders who plied the New England coast in the early seventeenth century. The chief sachem was described in 1621 as a "very lusty man" with "an able body, grave of countenance and spare of speech." He was not only a cordial host to the original Pilgrim settlers, but he also sheltered Roger Williams during that outcast's winter exile in 1636. Although he allowed Protestant missionaries to work among his people, he steadfastly resisted conversion to Christianity.

Massasoit, who led the Wampanoags for about a half century, is best remembered for his indispensable aid to the Pilgrims during their first year of settlement, for his great diplomatic skill and for his successful policy of peaceful coexistence with the English settlers during the forty years he dealt with them. The cornerstone of this policy was an agreement signed at Plymouth on March 21, 1621, between Massasoit and Governor Edward Winslow whereby each leader promised that he and his people would not harm the other, that they would give the other warning of danger, that they would assist if the other were attacked and that they

Chief Sachem Massasoit (Ousameuin), of the Pokanoket band, was the leader of the Wampanoag nation when New England's earliest settlements were established. In 1621, he celebrated a feast with the Pilgrims of Plymouth that has become the prototype of the modern American Thanksgiving. This representation is a model of Massasoit's statue atop Cole's Hill in Plymouth, Massachusetts, sculpted by Cyrus Dallin.

would work to maintain order and peace between the two peoples. This "league of peace," welcomed by the weakened Wampanoags, alarmed their rivals, the Narragansetts, but according to one leading scholar, "It established expectations that would have a profound impact on relations between Indians and English throughout the remainder of the century." This first treaty between these differing cultures addressed Massasoit as a "friend" and "ally" of King James, a signal to the Wampanoags that (at least at first) their relationship with the English was one of equality. Unfortunately, the English gradually developed the position that all Indians stood beneath them in the colonial hierarchy of power and property rights.

Although Massasoit is usually associated with the Plymouth Plantation, the Mount Hope lands in Bristol (Montaup) and the Indian village of Sowams in present-day Barrington were his places of residence because of his leadership of the Pokanoket band, the dominant sub-tribe of the Wampanoag confederation.

Upon his death in 1661 near his eightieth year, Massasoit was succeeded by his oldest son, Wamsutta, whom the English called "Alexander" (after Alexander the Great). When Alexander died suddenly in 1662, Massasoit's second son, Metacomet (called "King Philip" after Philip of Macedonia), became the grand sachem of the Wampanoag nation.

CHIEF SACHEMS CANONICUS AND MIANTONOMI

Canonicus (d. 1647) and his nephew Miantonomi (d. 1643) were the chief sachems of the powerful Narragansett tribe at the time when Roger Williams and other English colonists settled Rhode Island. The heart of the Narragansetts' strength during their "golden age" under Canonicus and Miantonomi was the tribe's close association with such smaller bands as the Pawtuxets, the Shawomets and the Cowessets on the west side of the bay that now bears the Narragansett tribal name. After avoiding a severe epidemic in 1616–17 that diminished the ranks of several tribes (especially the Wampanoags), the Narragansetts, under their two sachems, became noted among coastal Indians for the intensity of their religious rituals.

Under the uniquely arranged leadership of the two sachems, the Narragansetts rose from their home west of the bay to dominate the alliance among the Pawtuxets, Shawomets and Cowessets and to push

Chief Sachems Canonicus and Miantonomi—uncle and nephew, respectively—were the leaders of the Narragansett tribe when Roger Williams settled Providence. The original deed to Williams from Canonicus (who represented himself with a bow) and Miantonomi (who signed with an arrow) was executed on March 24, 1638.

the depopulated and weakened Pokanoket and Seakonke bands from the mouth of the Seekonk River. From there, the Narragansetts extended their influence up the Blackstone and Moshassuck Rivers to the domain of the eastern Nipmucks, from whom they obtained furs. They also controlled the flow of pelts and trade goods between Massachusetts Bay and the interior. Finally, they oversaw Indian-Dutch trade relations for the small Niantic tribe living in modern Charlestown, as well as for the natives of Aquidneck and Block Island. Because of their size and location, as well as the respect they enjoyed among other Indians as shrewd traders, devoted worshipers and committed pacifists, the Narragansetts, under Canonicus and Miantonomi, obtained their dominance through persuasion rather than violence.

In the winter of 1635–36 the Wampanoag chief Massasoit sheltered the exile Roger Williams, and in the spring the Narragansett sachems greeted him on the west bank of the Seekonk and allowed him to establish a settlement (Providence) on lands recently occupied as a result of the plague that had depopulated the Wampanoags.

The original deed to Williams from Canonicus (who signed himself with a bow) and Miantonomi (who signed with an arrow) was executed on March 24, 1638. It confirmed earlier verbal grants. "Not a penny was demanded by either," wrote Williams. "It was not price or money that could have purchased Rhode Island. Rhode Island was purchased by love." The first town boundaries established by this document (called the "town evidence") extended from a point just above Pawtucket Falls on the north, southwesterly to Neutaconkanut Hill and thence southeasterly to the mouth of the Pawtuxet River. The Blackstone, Seekonk and Providence Rivers served as the eastern boundary. In 1638, the sachems sold Aquidneck and Conanicut Islands to William Coddington, and in 1642 Miantonomi gave Samuel Gorton permission to settle on Shawomet lands in present-day Warwick.

Unfortunately for Canonicus and Miantonomi, intertribal jealousies and colonial greed would topple their empire. In 1643, Miantonomi (also called Miantonomoh) journeyed west to the Connecticut Valley at the head of a punitive expedition to chastise the rival Mohegan tribe for threatening a small remnant band of Pequots who were allied with the Narragansetts. The Mohegans repulsed the Narragansetts and captured Miantonomi, who was slowed in his retreat by his suit of armor. The Mohegan chief, Uncas, charged Miantonomi with the murder of an Indian and sent Miantonomi's case to the English authorities for disposition. The English commissioners (representing the settlements of Connecticut, New Haven, Plymouth and Massachusetts Bay) were covetous of Narragansett tribal lands, and this desire no doubt influenced their decision to return Miantonomi to Uncas in Norwich, where he was executed by Wawequa, the brother of Uncas. The fact that Miantonomi had recently been urging natives in southern New England and Long Island to bury their differences and unite in order to recover their autonomy and strength also sealed his fate with the English confederation.

The Pioneers

When Miantonomi was executed by blows from a tomahawk in 1643, the hope of Native American unification and successful Indian resistance to English Puritan hegemony was lost. The aging and infirm Canonicus mourned the loss of his statesmanlike nephew until his own death from natural causes in 1647. Prior to his demise, he joined with his nephew Pessacus, the brother of Miantonomi, in submitting themselves, their land and their possessions to the king, "upon condition of His Majesties' royal protection." The submission letter, dated April 19, 1644, was delivered to English authorities by Samuel Gorton, who had traveled to the mother country to secure imperial affirmation of the Shawomet Purchase—a deal that had earned the Narragansetts the wrath of Plymouth and Massachusetts Bay. This action gave them (or so they felt) a status of equality with the English colonists, "being subjects…unto the same king," and some protection from the New England Confederation. The Narragansetts relied on this status until they were drawn into King Philip's War in December 1675 as a result of a sneak attack on them by Plymouth Colony. Because they were equal subjects of the king, colonial officials could no longer rule on disputes between them and the colonists; such disputes could be decided only by a higher power.

Reverend William Blackstone

William Blackstone (1595–1675) was born in Whickham, Durham, England, the son and namesake of a wealthy landowner and poultryman whose surname was also spelled "Blaxton" or "Blackston."

Young William earned his AB and MA from Emmanuel College of Cambridge University in 1617 and 1621, respectively, and he then became an ordained clergyman of the Anglican Church. Independent minded, restless and at odds with the Anglican hierarchy, Blackstone joined an expedition organized in 1623 by Sir Ferdinando Gorges and his Council for New England that took him to the shores of Massachusetts Bay. When the leader of this voyage, Robert Gorges, the son of Ferdinando, returned to England, Blackstone elected to remain. He eventually established a residence in present-day Boston on the Shawmut Peninsula near Beacon Hill.

Boston's first English settler remained on this site until the religiously left-leaning Puritans (who wished to "purify" the Anglican Church of

This monument, near William Blackstone's grave, was provided by his descendants in 1889 and moved to its present location on Broad Street in Cumberland in 1944. Though Blackstone was an eccentric loner, a river and an entire region bear his name.

Roman Catholic "trappings") settled Boston in 1630 and the years thereafter. Because of theological and territorial disagreements with his new neighbors, Blackstone moved west in 1635 to enjoy the solitude and tranquility of a place he called "Study Hill" in the Lonsdale section of Cumberland, on the east bank of the river that now bears his name. This move gave him the unique distinction of being present-day Rhode Island's first permanent English settler. This location (actually acquired first by Plymouth Colony) was annexed by Rhode Island in 1746–47.

In these bucolic surroundings, Blackstone read from his extensive library, conducted missionary work and engaged in horticultural pursuits. He has been credited with developing the first American variety of apple and conducting the first Anglican religious services in Rhode Island by preaching to the natives and others who would listen.

In 1659, Blackstone married a Boston widow, Sarah Stevenson, who bore him one son. The eccentric cleric sometimes visited Providence for supplies, books and other necessities, traveling to and fro perched on the back of a large white bull. Blackstone died in 1675 just before the outbreak of King Philip's War, a conflict that brought destruction to his house and cherished library. There is no surviving likeness of Blackstone, but a large granite monument now situated on Broad Street in Cumberland near the Ann & Hope Mill and near his original grave site recalls his memory, as do the many places and business ventures in northeastern Rhode Island that bear his name.

ROGER WILLIAMS

Roger Williams (1603?–1683), Rhode Island's most famous personage, was born in London, the son of James Williams, a merchant, and Alice Pemberton. Remarkably, the precise year of his birth is unknown, and Williams himself gave conflicting accounts of his age.

As a very young man, he broke with the Anglican state church and joined the growing Puritan faction, to the dismay of his parents. Fortuitously, Williams attracted the attention of Sir Edward Coke, one of England's leading jurists, who employed him as a clerk and then arranged for his education, first at London's elite Charterhouse School in 1621 and then at Pembroke College of Cambridge University, from which Williams received his BA in 1627. He terminated his graduate studies in 1629 and became family chaplain in the household of Sir William Masham. There, he gained acquaintance with several notable Puritan families, including the Winthrops and the Cromwells.

Whereas Puritans initially aimed to "purify" the Anglican Church from within, Williams was moving toward complete separationism, even rejecting the elements of conformity that existed in the church's dissenting Puritan congregations. In 1629, he married Mary Barnard, a maid in the Masham household and the daughter of a Nottingham minister. During their long marriage, they produced six children and a host of descendants.

Infuriated by the High Church (i.e., "Romish") policies of the Anglican Archbishop of Canterbury William Laud, Roger and Mary left England aboard the ship *Lyon*, arriving in Massachusetts Bay in 1631. Almost immediately, Williams's radical views on religious liberty, separation and treatment of Native Americans embroiled him in controversy with the rigid Puritan leaders of the colony. He moved frequently, from Boston to Salem to Plymouth and then back to Salem. The latter settlements had Separatist beliefs, but they became annoyed by Williams's view that the colonists had no right to the land they occupied because their ownership was not based on purchase from the Indians. He was even so bold as to declare that the king's authority to grant such control rested on a "solemn public lie."

By January 1636, his preaching had earned him banishment by fiat of the Massachusetts General Court. As authorities prepared to place Williams on a ship bound for England, John Winthrop, who liked and respected Williams on a personal level, suggested that he flee to the area around Narragansett

Bay, beyond the bounds of Plymouth and Massachusetts. Taking Winthrop's advice, he left Salem in a wintry blizzard and found shelter with Massasoit and the Wampanoags—the tribe that had preserved the Pilgrims during the winter of 1620–21. Williams later wrote of Indian hospitality:

> *I've known them to leave their house and mat*
> *To lodge a friend or stranger,*
> *When Jews and Christians oft have sent*
> *Christ Jesus to the Manger.*

When spring arrived, so did Plymouth authorities to inform Williams and his dozen followers that they had settled east of the Seekonk River on land

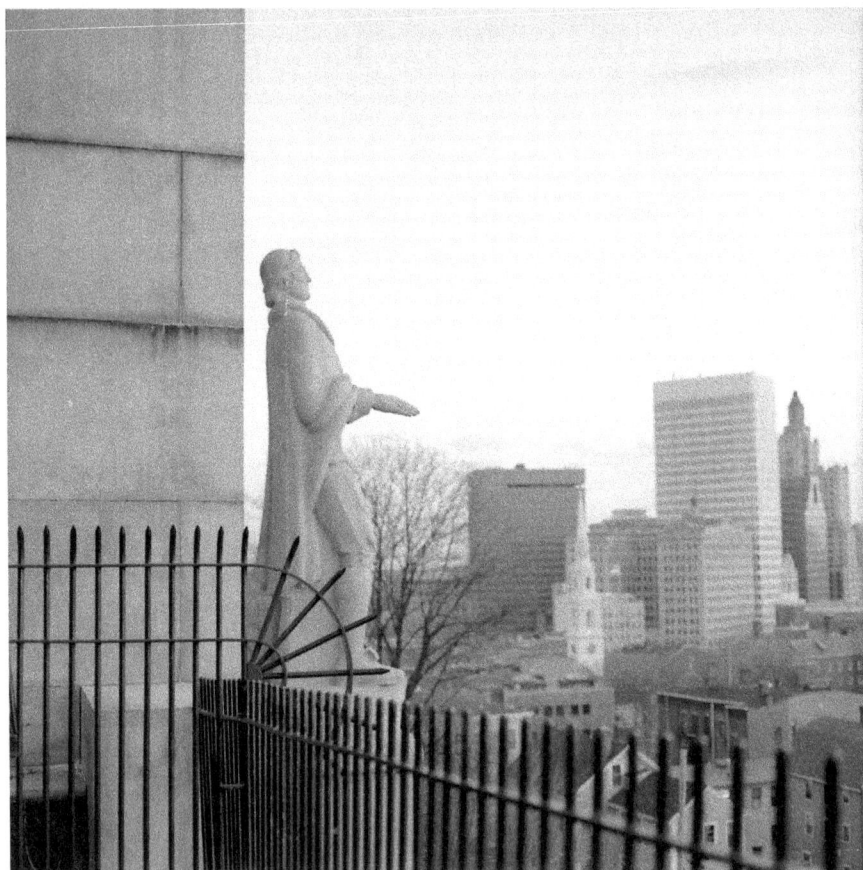

Roger Williams overlooks his city from Prospect Terrace. His fourteen-foot-high figure, sculpted from Westerly granite, was designed by Ralph T. Walker and Leo Friedlander for Rhode Island's tercentennial. It was dedicated in 1939.

claimed by Plymouth. To avoid further trouble, Williams uprooted, crossed the river and landed on Slate Rock (marked by a park on present-day Gano Street). Here, in mid-June 1636, they were welcomed by Narragansett Indians with the greeting, "What cheer, netop [friend]." The founders then bypassed this rocky, hilly site and paddled around Fox Point and up the "Great Salt River" to a spacious cove. There, on the east bank near a freshwater spring (where the Roger Williams National Memorial has been established), they laid out their settlement. Having "a sense of God's merciful providence unto me in my distress," said Williams, "I called the place Providence."

A relatively short biographical profile such as this can only outline Williams's forty-seven-year career as founder. He established his plantation based on complete religious liberty and separation of church and state (more on this key subject later); he obtained deeds in 1638 from Canonicus and Miantonomi (but not Massasoit) for his settlement, confirming earlier verbal grants; he established a trading post in the Narragansett Country in 1637 near present-day Wickford, confirming earlier verbal grants; and he helped to found America's first Baptist church in 1638 but left it a few months thereafter to become a "seeker" and a congregation of one.

When the surrounding colonies of Massachusetts Bay, Plymouth, New Haven and Connecticut joined in the New England Confederation and threatened his colony's existence, Williams journeyed to England to obtain the patent of 1644 from the parliamentary party. This document, secured with the assistance of Robert Rich, Earl of Warwick, was the first legal recognition of the Rhode Island towns of Providence, Portsmouth and Newport by the mother country. Samuel Gorton's Shawomet, or Warwick, settlement was included shortly thereafter, again through the intercession of Robert Rich.

In 1651, when William Coddington amended the patent by withdrawing the island towns from the new union, Williams joined with Dr. John Clarke and William Dyer to annul the Coddington commission and keep the tiny fledgling colony intact.

On his first trip back to England in 1643, Williams published the justly famous *A Key into the Language of America*. Printed in London by Gregory Dexter, who soon became a Providence settler, Williams's *Key* is the first English-language dictionary and ethnography of the Native American people. "Nature knows no difference," Williams wrote, "between European and American in blood, birth, bodies, etc."

On this productive visit, Williams also published *The Bloudy Tenent of Persecution for Cause of Conscience* (1644), a condemnation of Puritan intolerance and a defense of the right of each individual to worship God according to his own conscience, without interference from any civil authority. Forced worship, said Williams, had been historically the major cause of persecution and bloody religious warfare. Williams elaborated on this theme during his second mission by publishing *The Bloudy Tenent, Yet More Bloody* (1652), condemning the Reverend John Cotton's defense of New England Puritan policies. During the same visit, however, Williams interacted with such English Puritan leaders as Oliver Cromwell, John Milton and Sir Henry Vane.

In 1663, Dr. John Clarke crowned Williams's efforts and his own by securing the Royal Charter of 1663, a six-thousand-word document that contained a ringing affirmation of their theological and political beliefs and dealt a lasting blow to the designs of neighboring colonies to absorb Rhode Island. By then, Williams had successfully headed the colony as "president" from 1654 to 1657, while warding off external aggression and internal threats to union, and he now began to withdraw from public life. During the 1660s and early 1670s, he held minor town and colony offices, feuded with William Harris over issues relating to the boundaries of Providence and disputed with George Fox and the Quakers on political and theological grounds.

The transformation of the Antinomians to Quakers and the influx of the latter from England because of Rhode Island's famed freedom of religion gave the radical sect increasing influence on Aquidneck, especially in Newport, the colony's largest town. Williams disliked the Quakers because of their growing political and economic power, because they sided with William Harris and because he was convinced that they elevated themselves above Scripture by their belief of an "inner light." In August 1672, Williams, nearing seventy, rowed (or paddled) from Providence to Newport, reaching his destination at midnight to begin a raucous four-day debate with three Quaker missionaries on the following morning. In 1676, he wrote a long account of his experience entitled *George Fox Digg'd Out of His Burrowes*. Despite his intense disdain for Quakerism, however, Williams never advocated any governmental limitation on the Quaker form of worship or personal behavior.

The growing influence of Quakerism was not the only development that troubled Williams in his declining years. King Philip's War dashed his long-standing policy of peaceful coexistence with his Native American neighbors. Tragically, he became a victim of that conflict in March 1676 when a band of Indians, including Narragansetts, attacked Providence and burned his house to the ground. Even though the Narragansetts had joined Philip (Metacomet) after a dastardly sneak attack by Plymouth militia on their village in the Great Swamp, Williams was incensed by their action in putting Providence to the torch. After the war ended with a victory for the colonists and their Native American allies, Williams participated with other Providence men in rounding up and selling Indian prisoners of war and their families into a form of indentured servitude—but not permanent slavery, as did the neighboring colonies. This activity was a sharp and sad reversal of form for the man who had been a constant advocate of Indian property rights.

Williams continued to write and remained active in town affairs until his death in 1683. Samuel Brockunier, his most meticulous biographer, gives us the following account of his burial:

> On a fragmentary town record appears a reference to "The Venerable remains of Mr. Roger Williams, the Father of Providence, the Founder of the Colony, and of Liberty of Conscience." He was suitably honored "with all the solemnity the colony was able to shew," the militia firing their guns over his grave.

The exploits of Williams as Rhode Island's principal founder and his roles as theologian, public official, upholder of Native American rights and religious leader clearly establish him as the most important personage in the history of Rhode Island—but Rhode Island is a small place. Williams's influence transcended both Rhode Island and America. His views on religious liberty and church-state separation are global in significance. Hence, an examination of how those views were formulated (while difficult and tedious, like Williams's writings) merits extended analysis.

Williams's momentous experiment in "soul liberty" began in January 1636, when the Puritan magistrates of Massachusetts Bay banished this volatile dissenting clergyman into the winter wilderness. An avowed Separatist from the Church of England, the Cambridge-educated Williams was ousted for attacking the cornerstones upon which the Puritans' Bible commonwealth was built: the theology of the covenant and the use of civil magistrates to enforce that theology.

A vital area of disagreement between Williams and the builders of the Bay Colony was that Williams considered some religious doctrines propounded by the Puritans to be a prostitution of theology. His alternative to the orthodox Puritan approach was a cause for his exile. This alternative was a major element in Williams's notions of religious freedom and the separation of church and state, principles that found their expression in Rhode Island's basic law.

Roger Williams's challenge to covenant theology revolved around a method of interpreting the Bible, specifically the relation of the Old Testament to the New, which is called typology. His version of the typological method was based on a belief that everything in the Old Testament is merely a prefiguration of the New Testament, that each event in the history of Israel could be understood only when it came to fruition in the life of Christ and that the Old Testament lacked literal and historical content.

In its practical application to the lives of Massachusetts Bay residents, this complex method of biblical exegesis had important consequences. Among other things, Williams's method of interpreting the Scriptures was at variance with the historical mode of typological interpretation upon which covenant theology rested. Orthodox typology held that the Old Testament was simultaneously a literal *and* a spiritual work. On the literal level, Israel's scriptural theocracy provided the eternal pattern of civil justice; on the spiritual level, Israel, as the Promised Land, prefigured Christ. Orthodox typology thus intermingled the church and the civil state, and it supported the Puritan contention that the Christian magistrates of Massachusetts Bay could enforce religious conformity by basing their actions on similar powers exercised by the biblical Israelites.

Being of a purely spiritual nature, Williams's brand of typology disputed the Massachusetts Puritan belief that any political or social arrangement could be legitimized by reference to a similar arrangement described in the Old Testament. Specifically, Williams denied the right of the Massachusetts magistrates to use civil power to enforce religious conformity, a right claimed on the basis of Israelite precedent. It was Williams's contention that the events and the laws of Israel, having found completion in the New Testament, were without exception purely moral and ceremonial and were not to be emulated by seventeenth-century New Englanders.

Another crucial theological disagreement between Williams and the Massachusetts Puritans stemmed from their divergent views of the Ten Commandments. These divinely revealed injunctions were divided into two "tables": the first table (commandments one through four) was concerned with God and the worship of God and was called "ceremonial"; the second (commandments five through ten) was directed toward governing human relations and was called "moral."

Pointing out that judges and kings in the Old Testament state of Israel enforced both tables, Puritan divine John Cotton and his associates contended that this function continued to be valid. According to their interpretation, the task of enforcing the first table (worship of God) resided with civil magistrates and ministers acting in concert.

Williams believed that Jesus had abrogated this Hebraic system. He contended that Christ had set forth new laws of worship that had stripped judges, kings and civil magistrates of their right to enforce ceremonial provisions of the first table. These matters now belonged purely to the spiritual realm. "Soul liberty," to use Williams's phrase, pertained to the first table; it was exclusively an affair of private conscience, and the magistrate had no jurisdiction whatsoever in this area.

As a result of these interpretative efforts, Williams concluded that the temporal power exercised over the religious sphere in the Old Testament was merely the archetype of spiritual power in the New, and thus, whenever the modern state attempted to enforce conformity of religious belief, it was acting in an unjustifiable manner. That false assumption of power, asserted Williams, had led and would continue to lead to persecution and religious wars. Williams's obsession with religious persecution and its baneful effects on both spiritual and civil life occupies a prominent place in his thought and furnished the theme for one of his major works, *The Bloudy Tenent of Persecution* (1644).

The fiery minister's typological approach had liberty of conscience as its logical corollary, and it contributed substantially to Williams's dogma of separation of church and state. It is important to note that the theologically obsessed Williams sought this separation not to protect the state from the dominance of the church but to free the church and the individual conscience from the interference and coercions of the state. Williams's religious creed thus led him into the political sphere, where he was essentially a traditionalist who believed in stability and deference. As historian Edmund Morgan has observed, "So far as the political order was concerned, Williams had really only one revolutionary statement to make. He denied that the state had any responsibility for the only form of life which has absolute importance—the life of the soul."

Indicative of how strongly Williams felt about state domination of the church, in one burst of vituperation the polemical theologian asserted that such a condition would render the church "the garden and spouse of Christ, a filthy dunghill and whore-house of rotten and stinking whores and hypocrites." Obviously, Williams did not take the issue of separation lightly.

Among the conclusions that historians have drawn from Williams's earthy and passionate theological writings (which are collected, edited and published in nine volumes), the following seem to be the most significant: (1) any attempt by the state to enforce religious orthodoxy "stinks in God's nostrils" because it perverts God's plan for the regeneration of souls, and it is productive of persecution and religious wars; (2) God has not favored any particular form of government, and it is therefore to be inferred that forms of government will vary according to the nature and disposition of the people governed; (3) political and, especially, religious diversity is inevitable; and (4) the human conscience must be completely emancipated through the establishment of religious freedom and the separation of church and state.

Perry Miller, a noted historian of early American religious thought, has said that Williams "exerted little or no direct influence on theorists of the Revolution and the Constitution, who drew on quite different intellectual sources, yet as a figure and a reputation he was always there to remind Americans that no other conclusion than absolute religious freedom was feasible in this society."

In his *Religious History of the American People* (1975), Professor Sydney Ahlstrom supports Miller's view. Calling Rhode Island "the first commonwealth in modern history to make religious liberty (not simply a degree of toleration) a cardinal principle of its corporate existence and to maintain the separation of church and state on these grounds," Ahlstrom then observes that "Rhode Island seems to illustrate in an almost tragic way the...dictum, often voiced by historians of science, that premature discoveries are uninfluential." For Miller and Ahlstrom, Williams is to Madison, Jefferson and the Enlightenment-era framers of the First Amendment as Leif Eriksson is to Columbus: prior in time but lacking in influence.

Other recent historians of American religion and constitutionalism—including Mark DeWolfe Howe, Martin E. Marty, Edwin S. Gaustad, Glenn W. LaFantasie (editor of a recent edition of Williams's unpublished letters) and myself—hold a contrary view. According to these scholars, the founding fathers were well aware of the Rhode Island system of disestablishment and soul liberty, which was still intact under the same frame of government when the Bill of Rights was drafted and ratified; the guarantees in Rhode Island's famed charter of 1663 influenced similar grants of religious liberty in the proprietary charters of East Jersey, West Jersey and Carolina issued shortly thereafter; and Williams's views on religion and the state were distilled and reiterated by Algernon Sydney and other English writers of the Whig libertarian tradition with whom our founding fathers were quite familiar.

Williams was also associated with an Anglo-American Baptist tradition of separationism and soul liberty, drawing his inspiration from that tradition and strengthening it with his writings and example. Throughout the colonial and founding eras, as historian William G. McLoughlin has shown, the tradition was maintained, refined and modernized by the heroic determination of a coterie of lesser-known Baptist ministers and promulgated to the world of the founding fathers by the Reverend Isaac Backus (1727–1806), a prolific author and itinerant Baptist preacher who roamed the byways of southern New England spreading the gospel of separationism.

Perhaps Professor Martin Marty has said it best: the American church-state outlook has issued "chiefly from two parallel, often congenial, sometimes conflicting, and occasionally contradictory positions": the Rhode Island dissenting tradition, with its biblical base, initiated by Williams; and the eighteenth-century Virginia Enlightenment tradition, rooted in natural law and natural rights, expounded by Jefferson and Madison.

Despite Marty's balancing act, however, Mark DeWolfe Howe has effectively carried the historical controversy into the realm of current legal and constitutional jurisprudence. Asserting that the U.S. Supreme Court, "in its role as historian, has erred in disregarding the theological roots of the American principle of separation," he contends that "the predominant concern at the time when the First Amendment was adopted was not the Jeffersonian fear that if it were not enacted the federal government would aid religion…but rather the evangelical hope that private conscience and autonomous churches, working together and in freedom, would extend the role of truth." Citing Roger Williams's letter to the Reverend John Cotton, wherein the Rhode Island exile coined the metaphor "hedge or wall of separation between the garden of the church and the wilderness of the world," Howe maintains that "when the imagination of Roger Williams built the wall of separation, it was not because he was fearful that without such a barrier the arm of the church would extend its reach. It was, rather, the dread of the worldly corruptions which might consume the churches if sturdy fences against the wilderness were not maintained." Yet in making the wall of separation a constitutional barrier, the modern Supreme Court has failed to realize that "the faith of Roger Williams played a more important part [in the genesis of the First Amendment] than the doubts of Jefferson."

While one may endlessly debate the question of Williams's impact on the First Amendment, his influence on Rhode Island's basic law is indisputable.

All of the state's founding documents bear the indelible impress of his fundamental beliefs. The Providence town compact of 1637, that settlement's first frame of government, gave political power to the original "householders" but contained the all-important proviso that such control was to be exercised "only in civil things." A more detailed "plantation agreement" of 1640 reiterated this limitation; and the colonial patent that Williams obtained for the original towns in 1644 from the Long Parliament gave implicit sanction to the separation of church and state.

The culmination of this pioneering process, however, was Rhode Island's royal charter of 1663, obtained from King Charles II by tenacious Newport Baptist John Clarke, an important religious leader whose views closely paralleled those of Roger Williams. This document allowed the establishment of a self-governing colony wherein all local officials, from the governor and assemblymen to the viewers of fences and corders of wood, were either chosen directly in town meeting by the freemen or appointed on an annual basis by the elected representatives of the people.

The charter's most liberal, generous and unusual provision, however, bestowed on the inhabitants of the tiny colony "full liberty in religious concernments." The document commanded that "noe person within the sayd colonye, at any time hereafter, shall bee any wise molested, punished, disquieted, or called in question for any differences in opinione in matters of religion."

This guarantee of religious liberty was a vindication of Williams's beliefs and royal recognition of the fundamental principles upon which the Providence Plantation was founded: absolute freedom of conscience and complete separation of church and state. As Williams observed, this liberality stemmed from the king's willingness to "experiment" in order to ascertain "whether civil government could consist with such liberty of conscience." This was the "lively experiment" on which the government of Rhode Island was based.

Because such a free and open governmental system prevailed in seventeenth-century Rhode Island, the Colony House in Newport became a haven for Baptists, Separatists, Antinomian followers of Anne Hutchinson, Gortonians, Quakers, Sephardic Jews and Huguenots. In 1702, disgruntled Puritan leader Cotton Mather wrote that Rhode Island was a motley collection of all sects except Roman Catholics and true Christians (i.e., Congregationalists). This was the local legacy of Roger Williams.

As the Reverend Francis Wayland, a nineteenth-century Baptist president of Brown University, observed, the Pilgrims and Puritans sought religious liberty for themselves; Roger Williams sought it "for humanity." There are some men like Williams, added Wayland, "whose monuments are everywhere."

The Pioneers

ANNE HUTCHINSON

Anne Hutchinson was born in Lincolnshire, England, in 1591, the daughter of an English clergyman named Francis Marbury, who was censured by the Anglican Church for his Puritan leanings. (The Puritans wanted to purify the Church of England from any vestiges of the rejected Roman Catholic religion.) In August 1612, the well-bred and educated Anne married William Hutchinson, the son of a prosperous merchant. During the next twenty-two years, she dutifully bore her husband fourteen children. Then, in 1634, with the Puritans in disfavor because of the High Church leanings of King Charles I, the Hutchinson family set sail for Boston.

Anne's early religious training, her vigorous intellect and her restless and inquiring mind led her to take a leading part in the theological life of her intensely religious community. At first, she held informal meetings of women at her home, and on these occasions she would discuss the lengthy sermons of the previous Sunday. This activity was unobjectionable. Gradually, however, she began to lecture and to expound her own religious beliefs to audiences of sixty to eighty listeners that included men as well. This practice caused a furor.

Mrs. Hutchinson and the Reverends John Cotton and John Wheelwright preached a new doctrine that they termed "a covenant of grace." This view, held by a small minority of Puritans, asserted that salvation came principally through the individual's own personal awareness of God's divine grace and love. It challenged the orthodox "covenant of works," which was embraced by established, formal churches whose members gave evidence of their predestined salvation by their works and their status in the community.

Hutchinson and her associates denied that Christian freedom should be restricted by a need to seek evidence of election or salvation in obedience to God's law as interpreted by "hypocritical ministers." Since they placed their own intuitive interpretation of God's law above the civil and religious laws devised by man, those who believed in the covenant of grace were derisively labeled Antinomians, a word that comes from the Greek *anti* (against) and *nomos* (law).

It has been said of seventeenth-century religion that the Anglicans discarded the pope. The Puritans (Congregationalists) then discarded the bishops in favor of a formal, theologically trained clergy, but the Baptists were content with an ad hoc inspirational ministry to spread the word of God.

Hutchinson's view, emphasizing the direct connection between man (or woman) and God, undermined the authority and importance of the established religious and civil leaders of the Massachusetts Bay

Anne Hutchinson was the first significant white female leader in England's American colonies. This representation by sculptor Cyrus Dallin stands before the Massachusetts State House.

The Pioneers

Colony (who contended that society ought to be governed by Christian magistrates) because she discounted the need for a specially designated and highly educated ministry. In fact, the Antinomians (and their theological successors, the Quakers) dispensed with the clergy altogether and stressed the indwelling of the Holy Spirit and direct relations with God without the need for human intermediaries.

Such dogmas as Antinomianism and Quakerism shook the Bible Commonwealth of Massachusetts to its foundations. When advanced by a female (some labeled Anne Hutchinson a witch and the "American Jezebel"), they were even more pernicious. Hutchinson suffered excommunication and banishment for her beliefs, so she, her husband and numerous religious followers, including William Coddington, sought refuge in the Narragansett Bay region, an area that Puritans dubbed New England's "moral sewer."

Soon after her arrival at Portsmouth in the spring of 1638, she clashed with her coreligionist William Coddington, who held Indian title to Aquidneck Island in his own name. Through the intercession of fellow exile Roger Williams, Coddington, a prominent merchant of the Massachusetts Bay Colony, had purchased all of Aquidneck Island from the Narragansett Indians (who had seized it from the Wampanoags) as an Antinomian refuge in 1638. Joining with the equally rebellious Samuel Gorton, who later founded Warwick, Hutchinson ousted Coddington from power, so he went to the southern tip of the island and established the town of Newport in 1639.

Although bested temporarily, the very ambitious Coddington was not beaten, for within a year he had cleverly engineered a consolidation of the two island towns under a common administration in which he was "governor." Gorton and at least eleven other Portsmouth settlers responded to Coddington's resumption of power by plotting armed rebellion against him. These Portsmouth dissidents were ultimately banished from the island. Anne Hutchinson soon broke with the Gortonists over the use of violence, and she and her husband joined the Newport settlement.

Shortly thereafter, her fortunes plummeted disastrously. William Hutchinson died, her religious leadership waned and Massachusetts threatened to absorb the Rhode Island settlements. Disgruntled and disillusioned, she sought refuge in the Dutch colony of New Netherlands in 1642. In the late summer of 1643, her home (near present-day Pelham Bay, New York) was raided by Indians, who killed her, two of her sons and three of her daughters in brutal fashion.

The Massachusetts clergy rejoiced over the grisly murders. The Reverend Peter Bulkeley spoke for most orthodox Puritans when he pronounced this eulogy: "Let her damned heresies…and the just vengeance of God, by which she perished, terrify all her seduced followers from having anymore to do with her heaven." The Bay Colony divines considered Anne Hutchinson's death to be the symbolic death of Antinomianism, but the new religion of the Quakers found many recruits among her followers—William Coddington, her political rival, being the most notable.

Portsmouth's foundress was a remarkable individual. The double oppressions she faced—life in a male-dominated society and biological bondage to her own amazing fertility—were impediments to leadership that Anne Hutchinson successfully overcame. After her arrival in Portsmouth, and throughout the remainder of the century, women publicly taught and preached throughout Rhode Island; in part because of her example, the men of the colony protected the liberty of women to teach, preach and attend religious services of their own choosing. It would not be hyperbole to call Mistress Anne America's first great female leader. An indomitable mind, a zeal for equality and an energy that kept her constantly in motion indicate that this seventeenth-century prophetess was the archetype of the late twentieth-century woman.

Massachusetts has recanted. Admitting its unjust treatment of Mrs. Hutchinson, it commissioned the famous sculptor Cyrus E. Dallin to fashion a statue of her enfolding a child within her robes. That artwork now occupies a hallowed niche in the Massachusetts State House for passersby to view and ponder.

GOVERNOR WILLIAM CODDINGTON

William Coddington (1601–1678), principal founder of Portsmouth and Newport and governor of Rhode Island, was born in Boston, Lincolnshire, England. By his thirtieth year, he had achieved substance and position. In 1630, at about the same time as John Winthrop's arrival, he came to America as an assistant (director) in the Massachusetts Bay Company as part of the so-called Great Migration. In 1635, he was appointed to the colony's committee on military affairs; from 1634 to 1636, he was the Bay Company's treasurer; and in 1636–37, he served as a deputy in the General Court.

In a secular way, Coddington was similar to the shrewd and conservative Massachusetts Bay governor John Winthrop, but in religion he differed

Governor William Coddington's preeminence in the affairs of Aquidneck Island is indicated by his signature, affixed first, on the famed Portsmouth Compact of 1638.

from the orthodox Winthrop and embraced the spirit of Antinomianism, or salvation by grace. When another devotee of this doctrine in the Bay Colony, Anne Hutchinson, was hauled before the Massachusetts General Court in 1637 for "traducing the ministers and their ministry in this country," Coddington was bold enough to enter a protest on her behalf. Hutchinson was nonetheless banished.

Banishment did not at once overtake the influential Coddington, but in 1638 he withdrew to the island of Aquidneck, which he purchased from the Narragansett Indian chiefs Canonicus and Miantonomi with the help of Roger Williams. Here at Pocasset (Portsmouth), Coddington set up an Old Testament government of judge and elders, himself serving as judge. His name leads the signatories of the famous Portsmouth Compact of 1638. After the arrival of William and Anne Hutchinson and the contentious Samuel Gorton, disputes arose among these religious rebels, so Coddington and a number of his supporters left for the southern end of Aquidneck and founded Newport on May 16, 1639.

For a brief time, Portsmouth and Newport maintained a divided existence, but in 1640 they combined, formally declaring the new commonwealth a "Democracie or Popular Government" under the "Powre of the Body of Freemen orderly assembled, or the major part of them"; and "none [was to] be accounted a delinquent for Doctrine." Coddington was elected governor of this island commonwealth from 1640 to 1647. His steadfast aim thenceforward was to keep his colony of Aquidneck under his proprietorship and independent of the mainland settlement of Roger Williams.

In 1644, Williams secured from Parliament a patent uniting Aquidneck, or Rhode Island, to his own mainland settlement of Providence Plantations. Warwick joined that union soon after. In 1651, Coddington succeeded in having this document amended by obtaining a patent creating Aquidneck as a distinct colony, with himself as governor in perpetuity. This power play not only alienated Williams and Providence Plantations, but it also angered many of Coddington's own followers, who disavowed his action. When Roger Williams, Dr. John Clarke and William Dyer journeyed to England to protest Coddington's patent, Parliament annulled the Coddington grant in October 1652. At length, in 1656, Coddington reluctantly abandoned the plan to establish his own separate colony. "I, William Coddington," he wrote, "doe freely submit to ye authoritie of his Highness in this colonie as it is now united and that with all my heart."

Failure, however, did not attend him as a merchant. At Newport, prior to 1651, he built a "towne house," and he conducted a large Newport estate on which he bred sheep, cattle and horses, the latter for shipment to Barbados. Late in life, he espoused Quakerism and hosted that English sect's founder, George Fox, in 1672.

Having redeemed himself politically, Coddington was thrice honored with the governorship of Rhode Island and Providence Plantations (in 1674, 1675 and 1678). He was also thrice married and fathered thirteen children prior to his death in 1678; one of his children, William Jr., became governor of the colony from 1683 to 1685.

Dr. John Clarke

Dr. John Clarke (1609–1676) was the son of Thomas and Rose (Kerrich) Clarke. He was born in Westhorpe, Suffolk, in 1609, the fifth of seven children (according to a listing in the family's Geneva Bible) and the third of five sons, four of whom ultimately settled in Newport. He was probably married to his first wife, Elizabeth Harris, before he left England. Little is known of his education or formative years, but his knowledge of theology, Hebrew and medicine clearly indicates some formal schooling.

Clarke landed in Boston in November 1637, just after the General Court had taken its last rigorous action against Anne Hutchinson and her Antinomians. He boldly placed himself among the defeated supporters of the "covenant of grace," and they recognized him at once as a leader. He and other dissenters went immediately to Exeter, New Hampshire, and then to Providence, where he was courteously received by Roger Williams in early 1638. The result of this meeting and a consultation with the Plymouth authorities was a decision by Clarke and his associates to settle at Portsmouth on the island of Aquidneck.

On March 7, 1638, Clarke was one of eighteen who signed a compact at Portsmouth creating a new body politic. Although William Coddington, the first signer, was selected as judge, Clarke, as physician and preacher, was equally a leader, though he was not an Antinomian. Because of internal disputes about the governance of Portsmouth, a year later these two men and a few others moved to the southern end of the island, settling Newport.

Clarke's original relations with the religious denomination called Baptists are obscure. He may have had contact with Anabaptists in Holland; he may have been among those in Rhode Island who, according to John Winthrop, "turned professed Anabaptists" in 1641. However, from 1644 at the latest,

Dr. John Clarke, a versatile Newport physician and Baptist pastor, obtained Rhode Island's royal charter from King Charles II in 1663. It embodied the beliefs of Clarke and Roger Williams regarding religious liberty and separation of church and state. This portrait is attributed to artist Guilliam de Ville.

he was pastor of the Baptist church in Newport, and he thereafter became one of Rhode Island's foremost advocates for religious freedom and the separation of church and state.

The most unpleasant incident in Clarke's career was his 1651 trip with John Crandall and Obadiah Holmes to Lynn, Massachusetts, where he

The Pioneers

and his associates were arrested for holding a religious service and taken to Boston for trial. The specific charges against Clarke were unauthorized preaching, disrespect in the assembly of worship, administering the Lord's Supper to persons under discipline and denying the lawfulness of infant baptism. All three men were sentenced to be fined or whipped. Without Clarke's knowledge, a friend paid his fine of twenty pounds.

Later that same year, Clarke went with Roger Williams and Clarke's secretary, William Dyer, to England to void the patent making his former associate William Coddington proprietor of the Aquidneck towns and president of the splinter colony for life. After gaining recision of this grant, Williams soon returned to America, but Clarke remained in England as the colony's agent. In 1652, he published a tract in London entitled *Ill Newes from New England*, a pioneering treatise written to explain his emerging Baptist beliefs and to condemn the traumatic persecution he had suffered for conducting religious services during his 1651 missionary visit to Massachusetts Bay.

It is possible that Clarke returned to America for a short time in 1661, but he was in England in 1663 to secure the justly famous royal charter of 1663 from King Charles II with the influential assistance of Connecticut governor John Winthrop Jr., who had secured a similar self-governing corporate charter from the king in 1662. However, Connecticut's basic law contained no separation clauses—a purposeful omission that resulted in Congregationalism remaining the established church of Connecticut until 1818.

Rhode Island's liberal document, drafted in part by Clarke, enshrined his own views and those of Roger Williams concerning religious liberty and the separation of church and state. Clarke returned to Newport in 1664, triumphantly bearing Rhode Island's new basic law. The charter's famous phrases "lively experiment" and "full liberty in religious concernments" were due as much to the craftsmanship of Clarke as to the directorship of Williams.

While continuing to serve as minister and physician, Dr. Clarke was elected to the General Assembly from 1664 to 1669 and thrice held the office of deputy governor (1669–1672). He retired from political activity in 1672, a year after he married a second wife, Jane Fletcher, who died a little more than a year later following the birth of her child, who also died. Soon thereafter, Clarke married Sarah Davis, who survived him. Dr. Clarke left a will establishing a trust for charitable purposes, including "the relief of the poor or bringing up of children unto learning." The will resulted in the construction of a Baptist meetinghouse and much controversy in Newport over the distribution of Clarke's estate.

Recently, this pioneering but neglected apostle of religious liberty has become the subject of two biographies that recognize his equal role with Roger Williams in developing the American tradition of separation between church and state. Recent works by Louis F. Asher and noted colonial historian Sydney V. James now supplement the earlier biography by prolific Rhode Island historian Thomas Williams Bicknell. Despite this belated recognition and the recent formation in Newport of the John Clarke Society, the image of Roger Williams as colony founder, his interaction with leaders in both England and New England and his voluminous writings spanning nine published volumes ensure that he will always overshadow his like-minded Newport colleague Dr. John Clarke.

SAMUEL GORTON

Samuel Gorton was born in or about 1592 in the small village of Gorton, just outside of Manchester, England, a location that suggests that his family had some local prominence. Though Samuel (he spelled it with a double *l*) disclaimed a formal education, he was both literate and a linguist who could read the Bible in its original languages.

Gorton called himself "a citizen of London, clothier," in one legal document, but little else is known of his early life in England other than the fact that he became a religious dissenter who sought spiritual refuge in New England. He landed in Boston around 1636, where, as a harbinger of things to come, he was tried for heresy, fined and banished. Next he moved to the more religiously radical Plymouth Colony. Here he had his second brush with ecclesiastical authorities, who ordered him to leave. A freethinking man with a proclivity for disputation and a passion for the common law, Gorton next traveled to Portsmouth. There he again ran afoul of the settlement's leaders and was never admitted as a purchaser or a freeman.

His chilly island reception prompted Gorton and his increasing band of followers to try Providence. Even there, he stirred controversy to such an extent that four of the town's freemen—including Benedict Arnold, the first governor under the charter of 1663—willingly subjected themselves and their lands to the government of Massachusetts to bring a formal complaint

SIMPLICITIES DEFENCE

AGAINST

SEVEN-HEADED POLICY.

OR

A TRUE COMPLAINT OF A PEACEABLE PEOPLE, BEING PART
OF THE ENGLISH IN NEW-ENGLAND, MADE UNTO
THE STATE OF OLD ENGLAND, AGAINST
CRUELL PERSECUTORS,

UNITED IN CHURCH-GOVERNMENT

IN THOSE PARTS,

Wherein is made manifest the manifold outrages, cruelties, oppressions, and taxations, by cruell and close imprisonments, fire and sword, deprivation of goods, lands, and livelyhood; and such like barbarous inhumanities, exercised upon the people of Providence Plantations in the Nanhyganset Bay, by those of the Massachusetts, with the rest of the United Colonies, stretching themselves beyond the bounds of all their own jurisdictions, perpetrated and acted in such an unreasonable and barbarous manner, as many thereby have lost their lives.

As it hath been faithfully declared to the Honorable Committee of Lords and Commons for Forrain Plantations; whereupon they gave present order for redress.

The sight and consideration whereof hath moved a great Country of the Indians and Natives in those parts, Princes and people, to submit unto the crown of England, and earnestly to sue to the State thereof, for safeguard and shelter from like cruelties.

Imprimatur, Aug. 3d, 1646. Diligently perused, approved, and licensed to the Presse, according to order, by publike authority.

LONDON:

Printed by John Macock, and are to be sold by George Whittington, at the blue *Anchor,* neer the Royal *Exchange,* in *Cornhil.* 1647.

Samuel Gorton wrote and published *Simplicities Defence Against Seven-Headed Policy* (of which this is the title page) to expound his religious views and to condemn the Massachusetts Bay magistrates for their attempt to seize his Shawomet (Warwick) settlement.

against Gorton and his associates. Gorton, meanwhile, had moved to Pawtuxet in 1642, and in 1643 he moved once again, this time to an area south of Pawtuxet along Narragansett Bay. There he purchased a tract of land at Shawomet from the Narragansett sachems, over the objections of Shawomet chief Pomham and Cowesset chieftain Socononoco.

The Shawomet Purchase extended from Narragansett Bay twenty miles westward to near the present Connecticut border. This grant not only disturbed the tributaries of the Narragansetts (Pomham and Socononoco), but it also conflicted with the land claims of William Harris and the Pawtuxet proprietors who claimed Flat River in Coventry as their settlement's southern boundary. Hence, Gorton's opponents sought and received the aid of Massachusetts to oust this alleged interloper.

Desirous of a foothold on Narragansett Bay, Massachusetts sent a force of forty men to capture the Gortonites and carry them to Boston, where they were tried and convicted for contempt of authority, resisting arrest and uttering blasphemy. Most were released or given light punishment or indentured servitude, but Gorton and six others were put in chains and compelled to perform hard labor. After several months, they were also released, with orders not to return to Shawomet.

Once freed, Gorton, Randall Holden and John Greene sailed for England from New Amsterdam to appeal to the Commission on Foreign Plantations, which was headed by Robert Rich, the Earl of Warwick. They carried with them the Act of Submission of the Narragansett tribe to the English government, and they felt that this document would demonstrate the validity of the Shawomet transaction between subjects of the king. The Narragansett submission raised the decision to the imperial level.

Holden returned to America in 1646 with parliamentary vindication of the Shawomet Purchase, which Massachusetts grudgingly accepted. Gorton stayed for a while in England, where he published his famous tract *Simplicities Defence Against Seven-Headed Policy* (London, 1647), which denounced the religious leaders of Massachusetts Bay and Plymouth for their cruelties against the Shawomet purchasers and the Narragansetts. By the time he returned in 1648, Shawomet had been renamed Warwick in honor of its parliamentary protector, and it had gained inclusion under the patent of 1644 to round out Rhode Island's roster of four original towns.

Massachusetts persisted in its meddling until 1651, when it dismissed from its jurisdiction the four Providence men who had invited the Bay Colony's involvement. Although William Harris pressed his claim to the western area

The Pioneers

of the Shawomet Purchase until his death in 1681, the future of Warwick as a separate town was secure.

Upon his return from England, Gorton continued to reside, somewhat peacefully, at Warwick Neck with his wife, Mary Maplet, three sons and six daughters. He was repeatedly elected to town offices and to the colonial legislature. He also served as president of the mainland towns in 1651 and 1652 during the Coddington secession, since Warwick furnished traveling funds for the efforts of Roger Williams and John Clarke to rescind the Coddington commission.

Despite his long involvement in politics, Samuel Gorton was primarily a religious leader of a sect that was known to contemporaries as the Gortonians, who relied on his teaching and the five religious tracts that Gorton published. These contained an inscrutable array of beliefs that rejected any partnership between religion and the civil authorities and any outward trappings of worship, denied the Trinity, accepted the divinity of Christ, rejected a "hireling ministry" (i.e., a paid clergy) and asserted that he was the mere instrument by which the Holy Spirit spoke to his followers. No successor emerged, and after Gorton's death in 1677, his leaderless flock gradually drifted toward the Baptists or the Quakers.

REVEREND SAMUEL NEWMAN

The Reverend Samuel Newman (1602–1663) was a learned clergyman and the first prominent settler of present-day East Providence. He has not received as much acclaim as other Rhode Island founders because his village at Rumford, like the settlement of Thomas Willett at Wannamoisett, was beyond the boundaries of Rhode Island until the state annexed East Providence in 1862.

Newman was born in Oxfordshire, England, in 1602, the son of Richard Newman. As a youth, he entered the famous Magdalen College of Oxford University and took a special interest in religious studies. By the 1620s, Newman had become what was then termed in England a Nonconformist, meaning that he had embraced the tenets of Calvinism. In 1636, he immigrated to the Massachusetts Bay Colony to join other Puritan Nonconformists like himself. He first served as a minister in Dorchester and then moved to Weymouth in 1638.

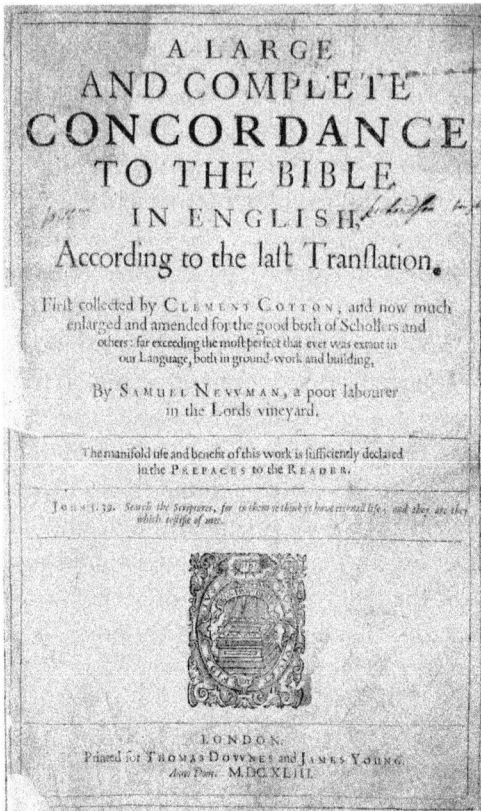

A LARGE
AND COMPLETE
CONCORDANCE
TO THE BIBLE
IN ENGLISH.
According to the laſt Tranſlation.

Firſt collected by Clement Cotton, and now much
enlarged and amended for the good both of Schollers and
others: far exceeding the moſt perfect that ever was extant in
our Language, both in ground-work and building,

By Samuel Newman, a poor labourer
in the Lords vineyard.

The manifold uſe and benefit of this work is ſufficiently declared
in the Prefaces to the Reader.

Joh. 1.32. Search the Scriptures, for in them ye think ye have eternal life, and they are they
which teſtifie of me.

LONDON.
Printed for Thomas Downes and James Young.
Anno Dom. M.DC.XLIII.

The Reverend Samuel Newman, the first Englishman to establish a settlement in present-day East Providence, was a noted Bible scholar, as indicated by this title page from his erudite biblical concordance.

During this period of ministry, Newman joined with Clement Cotton and others to prepare an alphabetical index to the key words of the Bible, the so-called Cambridge Concordance. Published in 1643, this work was the best concordance to the King James Version of the English Bible, and it earned Newman acclaim and respect in both Old and New England. It was reprinted many times, even as late as 1889, almost two and a half centuries after it was first compiled.

In 1644 or 1645, Newman led some members of his Weymouth congregation southwestward to present-day Rumford, Rhode Island, where they settled and soon established a church that survives today as the Newman Congregational Church. This area was called Seekonk (Seacunke) and was the subject of a jurisdictional dispute between the Massachusetts Bay Colony and Plymouth Colony when Newman arrived. Perhaps to his disappointment, Plymouth prevailed in 1645, but Newman was nonetheless influential in renaming the town Rehoboth, a biblical term meaning "wide or open space." This Plymouth Colony town at first comprised an area including present-day Seekonk, Rehoboth, eastern Pawtucket, East Providence and the northern part of Barrington, but the Newman settlement was confined to present-day Rumford.

Newman was Rumford's most prominent and influential early resident. He presided over the Congregational church there (showing little tolerance for Baptists) until his death in 1663. He also served for a time as the settlement's first schoolmaster as part of his community's pioneering program of publicly supported schools. One of Rumford's major thoroughfares and its most historic church are continuing reminders of Samuel Newman's prominence in the affairs of early Rhode Island.

WILLIAM HARRIS

William Harris (1610–1681) had a reputation among colonial Rhode Islanders for stirring up controversy. In his lifetime, he was the instigator of numerous lawsuits, and he was charged and indicted for tumults and high treason—and subsequently released. While Roger Williams and John Clarke may vie with each other for the title of "founder of Rhode Island," William Harris is a contestant for the title of "unfounder." Yet his role in the early history of Rhode Island was indisputably essential to the state's history, and it is inaccurate simply to write him off as an eccentric or a crank.

Harris came to Boston in 1631 aboard the *Lyon*, the same ship and voyage that bore Roger Williams to the New World. Like Williams, he settled in Salem and was one of the handful of adherents who gathered with Williams in exile at Omega Pond on the east bank of the Seekonk River in the spring of 1636, and he was one of those in the canoe greeted by the Indians at Slate (or What Cheer) Rock on that river's west bank.

Harris became a proprietor of Providence and an original settler at Pawtuxet. He also served several terms in the colonial legislature. These accomplishments were dwarfed by the land controversies that he instigated. At the heart of the many claims and suits instituted by Harris over the years was his disagreement with Roger Williams and the town meeting of Providence over the meaning of the Indian deeds defining the boundaries of Providence and Pawtuxet. Harris interpreted those deeds as instruments conveying all of the lands along the banks of the Pawtuxet River to the headwaters of its branches. Thus, thousands of acres were involved in his extravagant claim. Remarkably, during his lifetime he secured additional deeds from the Indians confirming his position.

Not only did these deeds extend the Providence and Pawtuxet boundaries twenty miles west of Fox's Hill at Fox Point in Providence, but also, because the south branch of the Pawtuxet extended into what is now West Warwick and Coventry, it overlapped the boundary of Warwick, which under the Shawomet Purchase extended westward to the boundary with Connecticut. The confusing lawsuits with Warwick and Providence

PAWTUXET
RIVER
ONE OF THE BOUNDS OF PROVIDENCE
MENTIONED IN THE INDIAN DEED
TO
ROGER WILLIAMS

This modern Pawtuxet signpost on the Cranston side of the Broad Street Bridge over the Pawtuxet River neglects to mention William Harris, the village's most prominent and contentious early settler.

over these land claims lasted from 1660 to 1678. At one point, Harris was jailed for alleged "treasonous dealings" with Connecticut. Although a majority of the Providence men agreed that the western boundary of the town was the Pocasset River, an imperial commission upheld the claims of Harris and his Pawtuxet proprietors against both Providence and Warwick in 1678.

To Harris's dismay, however, his court victory was thwarted by the town leaders of Providence, who ran a boundary line between the heads of the Pawtuxet and Woonasquatucket Rivers in such a way as to cut off Harris and his Pawtucket proprietors from virtually all of the land that they hoped to gain by the ruling of the royal commissioners. The outraged Harris made a final voyage to England in 1679 to gain redress, but he was seized by pirates and carried off to Algiers, where he was held captive until ransomed in 1681. Weakened by the ordeal, he went directly to England to resume his cause, but he died on the third day following his arrival.

Some writers have assessed his career as characterized by "land lust." Others have seen him as a supreme champion of individual rights. Williams denounced Harris for his "plot" to defraud the Narragansetts. Harris asserted that he was saving the town of Providence and the colony from the seizure of its western land by outside speculators. In any event, Harris added greatly to the early ferment that characterized Rhode Island as a place for the "otherwise minded" as he succeeded in enlarging the area of the tiny colony he helped to found.

RICHARD SMITH SR.

Richard Smith (1596–1666) was a major entrepreneur and by far the most important early settler of Rhode Island's present-day Washington (or "South") County. He was born in Gloucestershire, England, into a family of gentlemen-farmers. Because his religious beliefs tended toward nonconformity, he gave up his material advantages in England for a life in the New World. He came first to the Plymouth Colony and was one of the original purchasers of Taunton.

Soon thereafter, he met and befriended Roger Williams, and Smith's contact with Rhode Island began. Following Williams's lead, Smith opened a trading post in 1638 at Wickford in the Narragansett Country near a similar post recently established by Williams himself. As early as 1641, Smith purchased from the Narragansett sachems a tract of land that Williams described as

Smith's Castle, or Cocumscussoc (shown here), was built in 1678 by Richard Smith Jr. to replace an earlier large blockhouse built by Richard Smith Sr. in the 1640s that was destroyed in King Philip's War. The elder Smith and Roger Williams operated trading posts near present-day Wickford for commerce with the Dutch and the Narragansett Indians.

"about a mile in length and so down to the sea," whereupon Smith eventually constructed "a house for trade which gave free entertainment for travelers."

Smith's new structure was more than "a house for trade" and a place of lodging for travelers. A large, fortified building constructed of timber, it became known as Smith's Castle, or Cocumscussoc, after the Narragansett name for the area sold to Smith. He lived there with his wife and five children until his death in 1666. Though this building was destroyed in King Philip's War, the name was applied to the subsequent structure erected by Richard Smith Jr. in 1678 and is still in use today.

From this frontier enterprise, there evolved a prosperous country estate that figured prominently in the affairs of the colony. According to Carl R. Woodward, a president emeritus of the University of Rhode Island and an accomplished agricultural historian, Cocumscussoc's "broad acres and large herds set the pattern for other plantations which yielded shiploads of produce for the coastal and West Indian trade, and it was a center of social and religious life among the plantation families."

The house and the land, which at its greatest extent comprised twenty-seven square miles, passed by marriage from the Smiths to the Updikes, a family of Dutch ancestry, who held it from 1692 through 1812. The plantation reached the pinnacle of its prosperity in the mid-eighteenth century, but the economic and social disruptions that attended the War for Independence sent it into a precipitous decline.

Richard Smith Sr., the founder of this vast enterprise that he carved from the virgin forest, was an accomplished merchant and farmer. He bought out Roger Williams's interests in 1651, established an office and residence in New Amsterdam for trade with the Dutch and served as the principal economic intermediary between the English and the Narragansett tribe. As a farmer, Smith made the Cocumscussoc "plantation"—in the sense of the South's use of the term—a major agricultural enterprise, expanding through the years by additional purchases, and the first and most famous of its kind in the Narragansett Country.

Reverend Gregory Dexter

Gregory Dexter (1610–1700), born in Olney, Buckinghamshire, England, was admitted to the highly competitive and highly prized company of

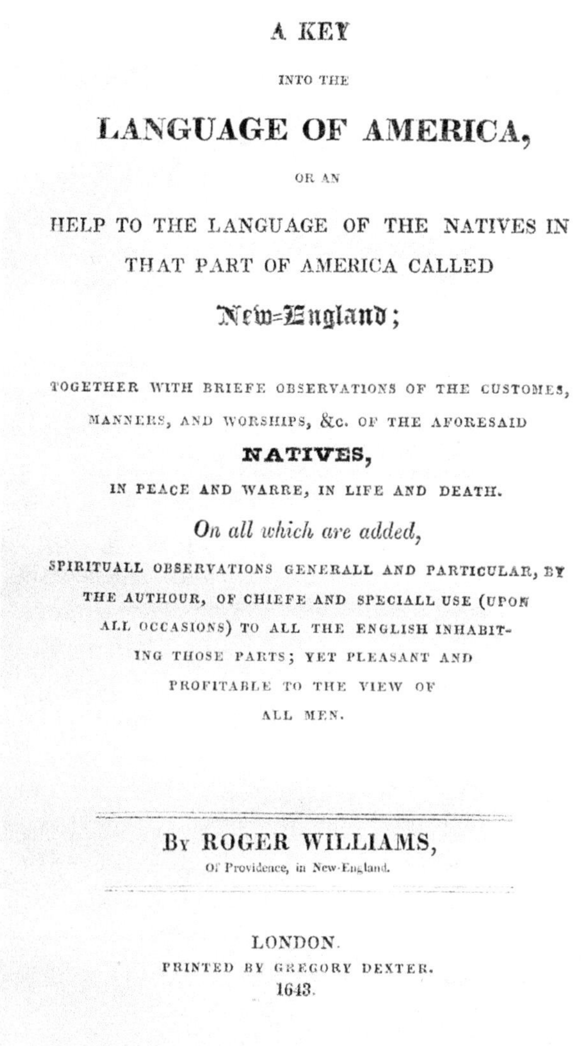

A KEY

INTO THE

LANGUAGE OF AMERICA,

OR AN

HELP TO THE LANGUAGE OF THE NATIVES IN

THAT PART OF AMERICA CALLED

New-England;

TOGETHER WITH BRIEFE OBSERVATIONS OF THE CUSTOMES,

MANNERS, AND WORSHIPS, &c. OF THE AFORESAID

NATIVES,

IN PEACE AND WARRE, IN LIFE AND DEATH.

On all which are added,

SPIRITUALL OBSERVATIONS GENERALL AND PARTICULAR, BY

THE AUTHOUR, OF CHIEFE AND SPECIALL USE (UPON

ALL OCCASIONS) TO ALL THE ENGLISH INHABIT-

ING THOSE PARTS; YET PLEASANT AND

PROFITABLE TO THE VIEW OF

ALL MEN.

The Reverend Gregory Dexter was not only a leading citizen of Providence, but also, before that, he was a prominent London printer who published Roger Williams's *A Key into the Language of America* (title page shown here). This book was the first English-language dictionary and ethnography of an American Indian people.

By ROGER WILLIAMS,

Of Providence, in New-England.

LONDON.

PRINTED BY GREGORY DEXTER.

1643.

stationers in London in 1639. Information on his early life is scanty, but his level of literacy and his professional success indicate that he received a sound education. Dexter became a printer to the famous English writer John Milton, and he also became the printer for Roger Williams. Among the works of Williams printed by Dexter was *A Key into the Language of America*. Although Dexter was one of London's finest printers, he was also a parliamentary partisan of the Puritan persuasion, and some tracts that he published brought down upon him the wrath of royal censors.

In 1644, Dexter joined Williams in Providence. Although he gave up his printing business, he became prominent in the town as the fifth minister of the First Baptist Church and an active participant in town meeting affairs. He seems to have had a hand in everything that concerned the fledgling community. Dexter's biographer, Bradford Swan, notes that leadership in Providence was sorely needed. Many of the early settlers were there because they wished to flee government. Such people were not inclined to help fashion a new government, even one that promoted participation and democracy. Dexter stepped in, negotiated land disputes and functioned as a town clerk.

He served the colony during several difficult crises. In one, he continued to hold meetings when Roger Williams had to go back to England in 1651 to quash an attempt by William Coddington to separate the island towns of Portsmouth and Newport from the colony and to rule them as governor for life. Coddington actually got the English government to agree to this arrangement, and Williams went back to undo it. Until Williams returned, successful in the mission, Dexter kept things together and even served as president of the mainland towns of Providence and Warwick in 1653 and 1654 during the Coddington secession. He was also one of Williams's staunch allies against the claims of William Harris in the Pawtuxet land disputes.

In one of his own landholding adventures, Dexter was granted a monopoly for the extraction of lime in what was then the wooded area in the northern part of Providence, and he began pit mines to remove lime. Colonial America had many uses for lime, not the least of which was the making of mortar for buildings. Dexter's Lime Rock quarry in Lincoln, with its extended activity under the Harris and Conklin families, is one of the oldest continuous businesses in America, dating back to the 1660s.

It is believed that Gregory Dexter died in 1700, near the age of ninety. A master printer and a champion of religious dissent and parliamentary power in Old England, in New England he was a colony builder and a supplier of materials for more substantial homes. In each case, his contributions had a lasting effect.

MARY DYER

Mary (Barrett) Dyer (ca. 1611–1660) was the wife of William Dyer of Somersetshire, England, with whom she came to Massachusetts in the

The Pioneers

Mary Dyer is depicted by artist Edwin Austin Abby as she is led from her trial before the Massachusetts magistrates to suffer martyrdom for defiant adherence to her Quaker beliefs. This painting is reproduced courtesy of the Social Law Library in Boston.

mid-1630s. According to Massachusetts governor John Winthrop, Mrs. Dyer was "a very proper and fair woman," and both she and her husband were well educated.

During the Antinomian controversy that rocked the Bay Colony in the 1630s, their open sympathy and support for Anne Hutchinson and the Reverend John Wheelwright alienated the Dyers from their orthodox Puritan neighbors. In November 1637, William Dyer was disenfranchised and subsequently disarmed because of his support of Wheelwright (who soon fled to New Hampshire), and later, when Mrs. Hutchinson was expelled from the Puritan Church, Mary Dyer defiantly accompanied her as she withdrew from the assemblage.

On October 17, 1637, in the midst of this religious turmoil, Mary Dyer gave birth to a badly deformed stillborn child and gave it a private burial. Not long after, the Dyers moved to Rhode Island to escape the hostile atmosphere of Massachusetts Bay. In March 1638, William Dyer became one of the founders of Portsmouth as a signer of the Portsmouth Compact. In that same month, Massachusetts authorities, on orders from Governor Winthrop, had the Dyer baby exhumed and published a lurid description of the child's deformities. Since Anne Hutchinson had assisted in the delivery, Winthrop stated that the "monster" was evidence of the heresies and errors of Antinomianism.

After more than a decade on the island of Aquidneck, Mary Dyer sailed alone for England in 1650. The reason for her solo departure has never been affirmed. Since she was a devoted wife and the mother of six minor children, including a newborn son, the only plausible explanation was her extreme religious fervor. In 1651, she was joined by her husband, who journeyed to London with John Clarke and Roger Williams to obtain a recession of the Coddington patent of 1651. At the conclusion of this successful mission, William Dyer left for Newport, but his wife remained until 1657.

During her extended stay in England, Mary Dyer zealously embraced the religious doctrines of George Fox, the founder of the Quakers, or Society of Friends. For her and many Rhode Islanders after her, including William Coddington, the similarity between Antinomian and Quaker beliefs made for an easy transition from one sect to the other.

As she passed through the port of Boston in 1657 upon her return to Rhode Island, Mary Dyer was arrested and imprisoned for heresy, but she was released upon her husband's entreaty. In 1658, as a Quaker missionary, she was expelled from the Puritan colony of New Haven. When several Quakers were imprisoned in Boston the next year, she went to visit them and to "bear witness to her faith," and she was again jailed. Banished from the Bay Colony on September 12, 1659, she returned to Rhode Island, but she soon made another visit of mercy to Boston to comfort other jailed Quakers. For this bold act of defiance, she was seized by the authorities and condemned to be hanged. At the last moment, upon petition of her son

William, the captain of a coasting vessel, she was reprieved and sent back to Rhode Island.

But on May 21, 1660, she once again returned to Boston and was again imprisoned and condemned to death. When offered her life if she would leave Massachusetts and return no more, she said, "Nay, I cannot; for in obedience to the will of the Lord God I came, and in His will I abide faithful to the death." Despite the supplications of her husband, she was hanged on the first day of June, becoming one of the four executed Quakers known as "the Boston martyrs." Eventually, Massachusetts repented by allowing a bronze statue of Mary Dyer by Quaker sculptress Sylvia Shaw to be placed in front of the state capitol.

MAYOR AND CAPTAIN THOMAS WILLETT

Captain Thomas Willett (1611–1674) was the principal early settler of Wannamoisett (present-day Riverside and northern Barrington) and the first English mayor of New York City. Willett was born in England and embraced Calvinist theology as a young man. Like many of the Pilgrim fathers, he left England for Holland, where Calvinism flourished, and like many Pilgrims he immigrated to Plymouth Colony. In 1636, seven years after his arrival in America, Willett married the daughter of John Brown, the most influential colonist on Plymouth Colony's western frontier, and in 1647, Willett replaced Miles Standish as captain of the Plymouth militia. Four years later, he joined his father-in-law as one of Governor William Bradford's assistants.

In 1660, Willett moved to Plymouth Colony's frontier town of Rehoboth (then consisting of Rehoboth and Seekonk, Massachusetts, and eastern Pawtucket, East Providence and the northern part of Barrington, Rhode Island). The place he selected for his settlement was called Wannamoisett, an area purchased from the Wampanoags by John Brown in 1645. From his base of operations, Willett became a trusted friend of the natives and an able negotiator. He purchased large tracts of land from the Wampanoags for Plymouth Colony, including the area of Sowams in present-day Warren, Rhode Island, and much of Swansea, Massachusetts. In 1661, he bought from Wamsutta, the eldest son of Massasoit, the territory that eventually became Attleboro, North Attleboro and Cumberland, thus expanding the

Mayor and Captain Thomas Willett of old Swansea, the first English chief executive of New York City, is memorialized by this monumental boulder in Riverside's Ancient Neck Cemetery near Willett's home. The stone was donated and set in 1913 by the City Club of New York.

58

territorial limits of the original Rehoboth. In addition to his land speculations, Willett was a merchant and a sea captain.

During the early 1660s, in support of the English attempt to take control of the Dutch colony of New Netherlands along the Hudson River, Willett led a contingent of Plymouth militiamen to Manhattan. When the English prevailed, Willett's knowledge of Dutch (gained from his stay in Holland and his numerous trading visits to New Amsterdam) enabled him to negotiate a political settlement with the last Dutch governor, Peter Stuyvesant, and to organize the new government of the colony (which England renamed New York). Having won the confidence of both English and Dutch settlers, Willett was chosen by Royal Governor Richard Lovelace in 1665 to become New York City's first English mayor. He served a second term in that prominent and sensitive post and acted as a member of the New York Colony's executive council from 1665 to 1672. When the Dutch temporarily retook New York in 1673 and his property there was confiscated, Willett returned to Wannamoisett, where he died in 1674.

Fittingly, the principal thoroughfare running through old Wannamoisett from present-day Riverside to Barrington bears Captain Willett's name. In addition, his important role in the history of New York City was recognized in 1913 when the private and prestigious City Club of New York placed a twenty-seven-thousand-pound inscribed boulder at Willett's grave in Riverside's Ancient Neck Cemetery. Willett's great-grandson, Marinus Willett, was chosen mayor of New York City in 1807.

CHIEF SACHEM METACOMET (KING PHILIP)

Metacomet, or Metacom (ca. 1638–1676), chief sachem of the Wampanoag Indian confederation from 1662 until 1676, ruled over a shrinking Native American empire on what is now Rhode Island's East Bay and southeastern Massachusetts. His English name and title, King Philip, were allegedly derived from Philip of Macedonia—a prophetic anointment before his involvement in the war that would bear his name.

His father was Massasoit (d. 1661), who befriended both the Pilgrims and Roger Williams. The initial cordiality between the English and native peoples soured after a long series of controversial land sales, lawsuits, religious conversions and double-dealings. Metacomet's elder brother

Chief sachem King Philip (Metacomet) is depicted in this wood engraving from the *History of King Philip's War* by Thomas Church (1717). Like all representations of early and mid-seventeenth-century Rhode Islanders, with the notable exception of Dr. John Clarke, this illustration is a posthumous artistic re-creation.

Wamsutta (also called Alexander) died in 1662 under questionable circumstances soon after being taken forcibly to Plymouth and held for sedition. Philip suspected foul play.

Upon assuming leadership of the Wampanoags, Metacomet made a number of important concessions to Plymouth Colony (though he angered Plymouth officials by giving preference to Rhode Island settlers over those of Plymouth in the sale of Wampanoag land). By the mid-1670s, when this humiliating policy of appeasement became intolerable, Metacomet urged other tribes to join a coalition for what he believed would be an inevitable conflict. "Brothers," he allegedly pleaded to his fellow natives, "these people from the unknown world will cut down our groves, spoil our hunting and planting grounds, and drive us and our children from the graves of our fathers."

A few small but violent episodes between the two sides detonated King Philip's War in June 1675. This confrontation cost the lives of more than six hundred colonists and several thousand Indians. In view of the region's population in the 1670s, the war was the most devastating conflict for loss of lives and property in American history. Philip failed to unite all of the local tribes, for many natives remained neutral or sided with the English, and once the uprising spread beyond the bounds of Plymouth Colony, other Indian sachems played leadership roles in their respective areas. During late 1675 and early 1676, the initial Indian offensive was successful, but by late spring 1676, the tide of battle had turned dramatically, with the English and their many Indian allies gaining control.

On August 12, 1676, the forces of Captain Benjamin Church ambushed Metacomet at his seat of power on Mount Hope in Bristol. Alderman, a "praying" Pocasset Indian, actually killed the great sachem as he attempted to escape. Colonial soldiers decapitated and quartered Metacomet's body and displayed the dead leader's head on a pole in Plymouth for many years as a deterrent to other rebels. Alderman was given Philip's severed hand as a reward.

Many of Philip's followers were either executed or sold into slavery in the West Indies. His wife and eight-year-old son suffered the latter fate when both were shipped to Bermuda in bondage. Today, Metacomet is deservingly honored as a native patriot who tried—in the manner of Pontiac, Tecumseh, Black Hawk and Geronimo—to preserve his own civilization and his tribe's autonomy in the face of overwhelming odds and the relentless greed and land hunger of America's white settlers.

PART II

The Stabilizers

1700–1763

JUDGE NATHANIEL BYFIELD

Judge Nathaniel Byfield (1653–1733), the most important of Bristol's original proprietors, was born in Surry, England, in 1653, the youngest of twenty-one children. He arrived in Boston in 1674 and soon gained wealth as a merchant. In 1680, the prosperous Byfield became one of Bristol's four proprietors, acquiring title to all of Bristol and Mount Hope Points in the southern part of the new town plus the northern portion of Poppasquash Neck. During his long residency in Bristol, he and his wife, Sarah Leverett, daughter of Massachusetts governor Sir John Leverett, had three children, who were raised at their Poppasquash home. In 1689, he wrote an account of the proceedings against Sir Edmund Andros and the aborted Dominion of New England that was published in London in the aftermath of the overthrow of James II and his dominion in the so-called "Glorious Revolution."

At various times in his career, Byfield held positions of influence both in Plymouth Colony and in Massachusetts when that colony absorbed Plymouth in 1691. His posts included that of chief judge of the court established in Bristol County. He also served as a five-time delegate to the General Court (the Massachusetts legislature), serving once as its Speaker. During the thirty-eight years he presided as chief judge in Bristol, Byfield also held the offices of judge of the Court of Common Pleas for Bristol

Judge Nathaniel Byfield was one of the four original proprietors of Bristol when it was founded in 1680 as a Plymouth Colony frontier town. This portrait of Byfield is by noted colonial artist John Smibert.

County, judge of probate for Bristol County and judge of admiralty for the Province of Massachusetts Bay, New Hampshire and Rhode Island. In addition, for many years Byfield was a member of His Majesty's Council for the Province of Massachusetts Bay. After the death of his first wife, Judge Byfield married Sarah Sedgwick in 1718. He died in Boston on June

6, 1733, at the age of eighty. Less than fourteen years after his passing, Byfield's town of Bristol and its environs were transferred from the royal province of Massachusetts Bay to the colony of Rhode Island, becoming the seat of Rhode Island's newly created Bristol County.

GOVERNOR SAMUEL CRANSTON

Samuel Cranston (1659–1727) was governor of Rhode Island for almost twenty-nine years, from 1698 to 1727, a tenure not only longer than that of any other Rhode Island governor but also exceeding that of any other chief executive of an American colony or state.

Cranston was the son of John Cranston, who was also a Rhode Island governor (1678–80); the grandson of James Cranston, a chaplain to Charles I; and a descendant of William Lord Cranston of Scotland. His mother, Mary Clarke, was the daughter of Rhode Island Colony president Jeremy Clarke (1648–49) and the sister of the colony's Governor Walter Clarke (1676–77, 1686, 1696–98). Thus, Samuel was well schooled in the art of politics and the beneficiary of his family's high social standing.

His first wife, Mary Williams Hart, granddaughter of Roger Williams, bore him seven children. According to tradition, young Samuel was captured by pirates and presumed dead. However, he escaped and returned to Rhode Island to find his wife (or purported widow) on the verge of remarriage. The wedding guests had actually assembled for the ceremony when seaman Cranston appeared to abort the nuptials.

In 1698, Cranston's family connections gained him election to the governorship, a post only death took from him. Fortunately for Rhode Island, the thirty-eight-year-old Cranston was equal to the many challenges facing Rhode Island at the time of his accession—royal displeasure, which threatened the colony's charter; boundary disputes; recalcitrant towns; defiant land speculators; and a colonial war with France.

Sydney James, the leading historian of colonial Rhode Island, speaks glowingly of Cranston's abilities and accomplishments in a summary worthy of extensive citation:

> *Such evidence as there is shows Cranston constantly at work. He was everywhere, serving as chief executive, president of the Council of War,*

chief judge of the Court of Trials, moderator of the Newport town meeting, presiding officer of the town council, promoter of civic betterment, committeeman for assorted tasks, spokesman for the colony in some delicate negotiations, and prime mover in four or five landowners' organizations. It may be fair to picture him as the doge of a nascent New England Venice… Governor Samuel Cranston presided over a transformation of Rhode Island from a beleaguered cluster of villages to a flourishing agricultural province organized to aid the growth of Newport's trade. He did not launch new policies as much as extend, elaborate, and carry out those that had been sketched a few years before he took office. His outstanding accomplishment, the key to many things that followed, was to bring his colony into a working relation with the imperial government in London while preserving its charter privileges. As he succeeded in doing this, it became possible to bring internal order to the colony and start settling old disputes with its neighbors.

Despite his record-breaking twenty-nine-year tenure as Rhode Island's governor and his aristocratic lineage, the only traces of Samuel Cranston are the municipality named for him posthumously in 1754, his signatures on colonial documents and this grave site in Newport's Common Ground Cemetery.

Cranston's role in stabilizing the colony is all the more remarkable because the position of governor was endowed with very few powers by the charter of 1663; constitutionally, governors were the mere agents of the omnipotent General Assembly. Nonetheless, certain chief executives—by virtue of their personality, prestige and capacity for leadership—transcended the limitations of the charter. Samuel Cranston was one of these. Like his predecessor Governor William Coddington Sr. and his colonial successors Samuel Ward and, especially, Stephen Hopkins, he temporarily transformed his office into a position of real power and influence. When the southernmost portion of the town of Providence was set off as a separate municipality in 1754, it was named Cranston in his honor.

BISHOP GEORGE BERKELEY

Eighteenth-century Rhode Island's most famous scholar was Irish clergyman George Berkeley (pronounced "bark-lee"), an Anglican essayist and philosopher, who renovated and resided at the beautifully preserved Whitehall Farm in present-day Middletown during his eventful stay in America from 1729 to 1731.

Berkeley was born in Dysart Castle in County Kilkenny, Ireland, in 1685 and educated first at Kilkenny College and then at Trinity College, Dublin, where he received a master's degree in 1707 and became a lecturer in divinity, Greek and Hebrew. In 1724, he was appointed the Anglican dean of Derry.

After periods of extensive travel in Europe, Berkeley crossed the Atlantic in 1729 to inquire into the condition and character of the North American Indians, a journey undertaken in expectation of a royal grant for founding a college for Native American youth on the island of Bermuda. By accident or design, he landed in Newport in the company of Scottish-born artist John Smibert, who had earlier visited Boston and was returning to America after a period of study in Rome and London,

So warm was the welcome accorded Dean Berkeley by the local Anglican community in Newport's Trinity Church and at St. Paul's in the Narragansett Country that Berkeley stretched his anticipated brief visit into a two-and-a-half-year stay. For his residence, he bought a one-hundred-acre farm and remodeled its modest house into a stately mansion, which he called Whitehall.

Berkeley was already famous as a great philosopher because of his early treatises expounding a Neoplatonic theory of reality called subjective idealism, a belief that contends that the world, as represented to our senses, depends for its existence on being perceived by the mind. Great crowds from all denominations attended his regular lectures at Trinity Church.

A mile south from Whitehall, on a rocky promontory commanding a view of the ocean, Berkeley had a favorite retreat where he kept a wooden chair and writing apparatus in a natural roofed alcove. It was probably here that he wrote two of his most celebrated works—*Alciphron, or The Minute Philosopher*, attacking those who based morality on "public benefit" rather than on a belief in God, whose existence, said Berkeley, "is the guaranty not only of the reality of the perceptible world but also of the moral"; and the poem "On the Prospect of Planting Arts and Learning in America," best remembered for the oracular line "Westward the course of empire takes its way."

From 1729 to 1731, Bishop George Berkeley had a brief but productive stay in Newport, where he contributed significantly to that town's intellectual life. This posthumous portrait by Alfred Hart, painted in 1831, is in the collection of the Redwood Library.

Still hoping that the grant of government funds for building his college would materialize, Berkeley continued his interest in the welfare of the Indians and made repeated visits to the Narragansett Country with Smibert, Cocumscussoc proprietor Lodowick Updike and the

Reverend James MacSparran, the Anglican rector of St. Paul's Church. Berkeley came to believe that Rhode Island was a much better place than Bermuda for his college; he especially liked a site on Hammond Hill in North Kingstown. However, the college grant was never made, and a disappointed Berkeley returned to Ireland in 1732 to continue his illustrious career as a philosopher of idealism and a critic of prevailing mathematical theory. In 1734, he was consecrated bishop of Cloyne, where he presided until his 1752 retirement to Oxford. He died in that university town in the following year.

The memory of Berkeley in America has been most conspicuously honored when his name was selected in 1866 for the University of California, Berkeley, and the city that grew up around this school. The trustees of the institution, originally called the College of California, were inspired by Berkeley's verses about "Planting Arts and Learning in America." The only flaw in their gesture was the mispronunciation of his surname.

Berkeley never forgot his sojourn in Rhode Island. He sent a handsome organ from England to Trinity Church and made valuable donations of Latin and Greek classics to Harvard. He also provided that upon his death, Whitehall and its library of some five hundred volumes should go to Yale College. At that time, both Harvard and Yale were under Congregational auspices. Berkeley's ecumenism and love of learning transcended sectarian boundaries.

JAMES AND ANN (SMITH) FRANKLIN

James Franklin (1697–1735) was the first of ten children born to Josiah Franklin and Abiah Folger of Boston. He learned the printing trade in England and then returned to America, where in 1721 he began publication of the controversial and independent *New England Courant*, a newspaper disrespectful of civil and ecclesiastical policies. Young Benjamin Franklin—child number eight in the family—also worked on this paper until 1723 as an apprentice to his brother, who treated him harshly. Like many adopted Rhode Islanders, James Franklin ran afoul of the Massachusetts authorities, and having been jailed for a month for his opinions, he left Boston in 1726 for Newport, the home of his brother John, a tallow chandler.

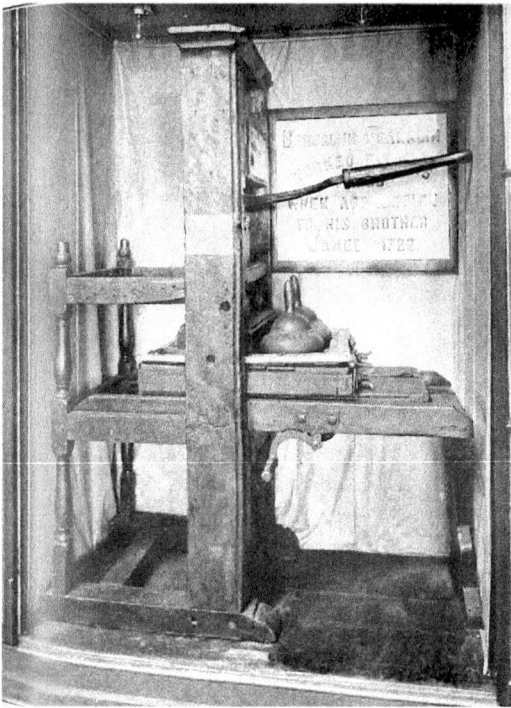

James and Ann (Smith) Franklin brought this printing press from Boston to Newport in 1726 after constant disputes over newspaper content with Massachusetts authorities. Younger brother Benjamin, who had been apprenticed on this machine, opted for Philadelphia. This photo is reproduced courtesy of the Massachusetts Charitable Mechanics Association.

In 1727, Franklin and his wife, the former Ann Smith (1696–1763), set up Rhode Island's first printing press. In 1732, he issued the *Rhode Island Gazette*, the colony's first newspaper, but it was discontinued on May 24, 1733. Franklin also printed books, pamphlets and almanacs, sometimes using the pen name "Poor Robin," which may have inspired his brother's "Poor Richard."

When James Franklin died on February 4, 1735, his thirty-eighth birthday, leaving behind four children (one had preceded him in death), the printing shop was continued under the auspices of Ann Franklin, whose imprint appeared as "The Widow Franklin." She also printed books, almanacs and pamphlets, as well as five hundred copies of the colony's *Acts and Laws* (the Digest of 1745) in a folio edition.

Ann Franklin was eventually joined by her son, James Jr., who had apprenticed in Philadelphia with his uncle Benjamin. In June 1758, James Franklin Jr. published the first issue of the *Newport Mercury*, which became one of colonial America's important newspapers. When he died in 1762, his mother once again took over the management of her printing business, which she carried on for another year until her own death. The Franklins of Newport were pioneers in the American publishing industry and exerted a strong influence on public opinion in colonial Rhode Island.

WILLIAM CLAGGETT SR.

William Claggett (1696–1749) was born in England or Wales, the son of a baker about whom little else is known. As a youth, he migrated with his family to Boston, served an apprenticeship to clockmaker Benjamin Bagnall and, at age nineteen, married Mary Armstrong in a ceremony presided over by Cotton Mather. His son William, who also became a noted clockmaker, was born in 1715.

About 1716, Claggett came to Newport, where he lived and worked for the next thirty-three years until his death in 1749 at his home at 16 Bridge Street. In cosmopolitan Newport, Claggett gained recognition not only as a clock- and watchmaker and repairer but also as an organ builder, engraver, compass maker, printer, lecturer, author, notary public, founder of a fire company and experimenter in the new field of electricity.

In the 1740s, Claggett built a large electrical machine that he used for experimental purposes. Many curious New Englanders paid to view the device, and Claggett donated much of the large amount of money raised from the machine's exhibition to charitable causes. According to an account of this venture by Dr. Arthur Ross, Claggett probably demonstrated the machine to longtime acquaintance Benjamin Franklin, who later improved on Claggett's technology. Historian Ross even credits Claggett with arousing Franklin's interest in electricity. The noted Philadelphian, the younger brother and one-time apprentice of Newport printer James Franklin, began his experiments with electricity in 1746, when Claggett was exhibiting his invention to the citizens of Newport and Boston.

Today, Claggett is best remembered as the premier clockmaker of colonial Rhode Island.

William Claggett Sr. crafted this tall case clock about 1730. It is now owned by Gail C. Conley and graces her Bristol Point home. The timepiece faces southward down the bay toward the Point section of Newport, where Claggett lived and worked.

Most notable are his tall case (or grandfather) clocks, which today command high prices. At the turn of this century, George Richardson, then secretary of the Newport Historical Society and a descendant of Claggett, listed eighteen surviving William Claggett clocks, all in the immediate area of Newport. Another tally in 1975 lists fifty-one signed by William Claggett, but whether by William I, William II (his son) or William III (his grandson) is uncertain. In addition to these, Claggett made the original tower clock for Newport's Trinity Church. Evidence of Claggett's craftsmanship as a clockmaker can be viewed today at both the Newport Historical Society and the Rhode Island Historical Society, where Claggett clocks are on display. An article by Richard L. Champlin entitled "William Claggett and His Clockmaking Family," published in *Newport History*, was enlarged and reprinted in 1976 in the *Bulletin of the National Association of Watch and Clock Collectors*.

REVEREND JOHN CALLENDER

The Reverend John Callender (1706–1748) became the first historian of Rhode Island in 1738 when he wrote a work to commemorate the colony's centennial. Not surprisingly, he viewed his topic through a religious prism; surprisingly, he thought the arrival of William Coddington, Anne Hutchinson, Dr. John Clarke and other Aquidneck settlers in 1638 truly launched the colony. This era's most authoritative historian, Sydney James, observes that

> *in Callender's day, common sense could readily find reasons for assigning primacy to these people. Their towns on the island of Aquidneck, Newport, and Portsmouth, were still the center of wealth, population, culture, and government in the colony.*

Rhode Island's first historian was born in Boston, the son of Priscilla Man and John Callender and the grandson of the Reverend Ellis Callender, pastor of that town's First Baptist Church from 1708 to 1726. Young John entered Harvard College at the age of thirteen with the assistance of income provided by Thomas Hollis, a London Baptist, who had endowed two professorships at the school and also supplied Harvard with scholarship

The Stabilizers

Commissioned in 1745 by Henry Collins, a wealthy Newport merchant, this impressive oil-on-canvas portrait of the Reverend John Callender was painted by the itinerant artist Robert Feke. It was donated to the Rhode Island Historical Society in 1847 by Henry Bull of Newport.

funds. Upon graduation in 1726 with a master's degree, Callender joined his grandfather's congregation and soon obtained a license to preach. In August 1728, he began his ministry by teaching in Swansea at the oldest Baptist church in Massachusetts, an assembly that dated from 1663. There he remained until February 1730. While a resident of that former Plymouth Colony town, Callender met Elizabeth Hardin. The couple soon married and eventually had three sons and three daughters, one of whom—Mary—became a noted preacher in the Society of Friends.

In October 1731, at the age of twenty-five, Callender was ordained to the regular ministry by his uncle Elisha and became pastor of the Baptist church in Newport, founded by Dr. John Clarke—the second oldest church of that faith in colonial America. He held this prestigious post for nearly seventeen years until his death.

During his pastorate, Callender became one of Newport's religious, civic and intellectual leaders and a member of the local library and philosophical society. This organization, the Society for Promoting Virtue and Knowledge by a Free Conversation, became the basis for the Redwood Library. Among his civic posts were schoolmaster, an office to which he was elected by the citizens of Newport in 1746, and service on a legislative committee to revise and print the colony's laws. This committee produced the *Acts and Laws* (Digest of 1745) published by Ann Franklin. Callender's gentle, ecumenical and nonconfrontational demeanor made him popular and well liked in Newport and beyond.

Though he wrote several widely circulated sermons, Callender's major effort was *An Historical Discourse on the Civil and Religious Affairs of the Colony of Rhode Island and Providence Plantations in New England, In America*, published by a Boston printer in 1739, one year after its completion. In the Baptist tradition, this 130-page narrative extolled the concepts of religious liberty and church-state separation on which the colony was founded. At one point, in his so-called "Century Sermon," Callender remarked that "the surest way to preserve and enjoy our Charter privileges, is to divide the posts of honor, trust, and profit among all [religious] persuasions indifferently; and, in general, to prefer those gentlemen, of whatever religious opinions...that are best qualified to serve the public...and to suffer no one religious sect to monopolize the places of power and authority." At this time, ironically, the Rhode Island body politic was governed by a 1719 statute that barred Roman Catholics and those of the Jewish faith from voting or holding office. That law was repealed for Catholics in 1783 and for Jews in 1798. Callender's discourse was a veiled rebuke to the prevailing discriminatory system.

Callender's interest in history also led him to collect historical documents relating to the Baptist denomination, and his research material was a useful source of information for the Reverend Isaac Backus when the latter wrote his history of the Baptists in New England.

The Reverend Callender was especially noteworthy for his harmonious relationship with Congregationalists in both Newport and Boston. He was a close friend and classmate of Samuel Mather, grandson of Increase Mather, who had persecuted the earliest Baptists in Massachusetts. He preached a tolerant, non-strident form of theology referred to by historians of American religion as "Old Light," a view that identified with inherited institutions and saw preaching as a way to preserve the social order. According to historian William Joyce, "the importance of Callender's writing lay in its marking a change from conflict between Baptists and Congregationalists to one among groups within both churches." Education and socioeconomic standing became the factors within each religious group that produced conflicting attitudes toward social and theological issues. Clearly, the educated and urbane Callender approached religion differently from most of his rural Baptist counterparts, who were swept up in the contemporary revival called the Great Awakening.

The Stabilizers

John Callender died on January 26, 1748, after a long illness and was interred at Newport's Common Burial Ground. His passing produced several eloquent eulogies, not only by Newporters but by the Boston press as well. The *Gazette* described him accurately as a "gentleman of…natural accomplishments, and extensive learning; of the greatest integrity and modesty," and the *Boston Evening Post* remembered him as a man of "superior good sense and very extensive knowledge who was an entire stranger to cunning and artifice."

REVEREND DR. JAMES MACSPARRAN

Dr. James MacSparran (1693–1757) was born in County Derry, Ireland, of Presbyterian parents who had emigrated from Scotland. He earned a master's degree at the University of Glasgow and then studied for the Presbyterian ministry. In 1718, he came to America from his native Ireland and served for a year in Bristol as pastor of the Congregational Church, a sect akin to Presbyterianism in its Calvinist theology. But a dispute with Boston Congregational leader Cotton Mather clouded his appointment, and as a result he changed his church affiliation upon his return to Ireland.

When MacSparran again set foot in Rhode Island in December 1721, it was as a presbyter of the Church of England, assigned as a missionary of the Society for the Propagation of the Gospel in Foreign Parts to the Narragansett County of Southern Rhode Island and other outposts. MacSparran's parish church was Old St. Paul's, founded in 1707 about five miles south of Smith's Castle at Cocumscussoc, which moved to its present site in Wickford in 1800.

For the next thirty-six and a half years, the learned Anglican clergyman was a dominant religious and intellectual influence in South County. In addition to his pastoral work, MacSparran became a gentleman farmer, a practicing physician and a tutor whose students included Thomas Clap, later president of Yale. On his visit to England in 1736, his achievements prompted Oxford University to confer on him an honorary doctorate of sacred theology.

MacSparran was the author of a series of analytical letters to friends in Ireland graphically depicting the American colonies in their various aspects—environmental, political, economic and religious. These letters were published in 1753 under the title *America Dissected*, and they discouraged emigration. MacSparran kept a diary, a document rich in human interest, some of which (the entries for 1743 to 1745 and 1751) has survived. This narrative is one of the few extant day-to-day records of farming in colonial New England, and it is regarded as the best written record of slave labor on the plantations of southern Rhode Island.

A major blemish on MacSparran's record is that he held slaves, as did the other major South County landholders. In mitigation of this fact is the observation of historian Carl R. Woodward that

> *a perusal of his diary leaves one with the impression that in some respects Dr. MacSparran's slaves commanded nearly as much of his interest and concern as did his parishioners. Actually he counted not only his slaves but those belonging to other parish families as members of his flock, deserving of his ministrations, both medical and spiritual.*

In 1722, MacSparran married Hannah Gardiner, who became his helpmate until her death in London from smallpox in June 1755 during one of the MacSparrans' visits to England. Her passing had a profound impact on his outlook and his health, and having returned to St. Paul's broken in spirit, he died there in December 1757.

The Reverend Dr. James MacSparran, spiritual leader of the Anglicans of the Narragansett Country, was of Scottish ancestry. His family immigrated to the village of Dungiven in the county of Derry in the north of Ireland. This portrait by John Smibert is in the possession of Bowdoin College.

The Stabilizers

MacSparran was an imposing speaker and had a commanding presence. Tall and portly (he reputedly weighed nearly three hundred pounds), sometimes dominating in manner and given to certain foibles, he has been described by Professor Woodward as "the most able divine sent to this country by the Society [for the Propagation of the Gospel]."

SAMUEL CASEY

Samuel Casey (1724–?) was born in Newport, the descendant of Thomas Casey, an Irishman who allegedly fled his country in the 1640s to escape English persecution. Little is known of Casey's early life or his training for the craft of silversmithing, other than that he held an apprenticeship to Jacob Hurd in Boston. In 1745, he was admitted as a freeman of the newly created town of Exeter, a rural area that had been set off from North Kingstown in 1743.

For several years, Casey practiced his craft in Exeter, fashioning work that has been described by experts as much more imaginative than that of most of his contemporaries. About 1750, he relocated to the South Kingstown village of Little Rest (now known as Kingston), where he entered into a partnership with his brother, Gideon. Here he married Martha Martin.

Little Rest was a vibrant village that had become the business center of the region and serviced the needs of the nearby Narragansett plantations. Casey's home and shop on the main street gave his customers easy access and allowed him to supplement his income by opening a dry goods store. In September 1764, however, disaster struck: Casey's house burned as a result of a fire sparked by his forge. The flames destroyed his expensive furnishings and many of the tools of his craft.

Casey rebuilt his home and studio, but he turned his great skill to counterfeiting (then called "moneymaking") to recoup his losses more quickly. This crime was a natural one for silversmiths, because they possessed the technical skills to make dies for printing fake money. In fact, silversmiths were often hired by colonial governments to make the dies for legal tender.

Despite his legal and illegal activities, in March 1770, Casey submitted a petition for insolvency to the General Assembly, signed by twenty-seven of his creditors. A subsequent investigation of his finances disclosed that he was the head of a group of silversmith counterfeiters operating from the attic of his Little Rest home, where authorities found a press and dies. Casey

Samuel Casey, colonial Rhode Island's foremost silversmith, led a colony of fellow craftsmen in the South Kingstown village of Little Rest (now known as Kingston). This tankard by Casey is part of a remarkable collection of early American silver assembled by prominent Newport attorney Cornelius C. Moore and donated to Providence College. Alice Hauck edited and published a catalogue of the collection in 1980 entitled *American Silver, 1670–1830*. It includes many works by Casey.

was arrested, along with four accomplices, and tried in October 1770 in the King's County Courthouse in Little Rest.

After he had recanted his confession, a friendly jury found him not guilty. This annoyed the five-member judicial panel, so it validated the confession and sent the jury back to deliberate. Casey was then convicted and sentenced to hang. His four associates got sentences requiring ear cropping, branding, the pillory or public whipping. On the night before his scheduled execution, Casey was freed by a mob of his friends and neighbors, and he fled Rhode Island, never to return.

Lawyer-historian Christian McBurney, the leading modern historian of Kingston, discovered a petition for amnesty presented to the General Assembly by Casey's wife in 1779, a document asserting that Casey "wandered in exile nine years forlorn and forsaken and destitute of every means of support…separated from his wife and offspring." Amazingly, the legislature voted to pardon the silversmith, but Casey never took advantage of that pardon. McBurney states that a Canadian descendant of Casey recollected that Samuel had been a Loyalist during the War for Independence and died in that conflict. McBurney theorizes that "this report is somewhat supported by evidence that Samuel Casey's son fought as a Tory and after the war fled to Canada."

One thing is certain: Casey was the most accomplished silversmith of early Rhode Island. A modern collector has stated that Casey was second only to Paul Revere in the skill that he brought to his craft.

The Stabilizers

His teapots, creamers, tankards and porringers are highly prized and featured in all of the major museums around the country that celebrate the skills of colonial American craftsmen. Casey's works demonstrate the Queen Anne and rococo styles, the first characterized by simple forms that rely on contour and plain surfaces with little decoration, and the latter emphasizing detail and surface ornamentation. A sizable number of Casey's pieces are reproduced in Alice Hauck's *American Silver, 1670–1830* (1980), a catalogue of the fine silver collection of the late Newport attorney Cornelius C. Moore.

PETER HARRISON

Peter Harrison (1716–1775) was born in Yorkshire, England, to Quaker parents and came to Newport in 1738 on a merchant vessel. Upon arrival, he worked with his older brother, Joseph, in both agriculture and trade, dealing in wines, rum, molasses and mahogany under the auspices of Newport merchant John Banister.

According to certain accounts, he received some architectural training during a stay in England in the early 1740s at a private studio-school sponsored by an English aristocrat. This school, like others, drew from the works of the masters, using pattern books and sponsoring grand tours of Italy and Greece. It is known that on a voyage from Livorno, Italy, to New England in early 1744, during King George's War with France, he was captured by a French privateer and imprisoned in the famous French fortress of Louisbourg in Nova Scotia. Here he was given preferred treatment, but he repaid his captors by doing drawings of the fort and its defenses, which he hid in his clothing upon his relatively quick release in a prisoner exchange. These plans were used by Massachusetts governor William Shirley and his military commanders, William Pepperrell and Admiral Peter Warren (for whom the Rhode Island town is named), to wage a successful assault on Louisbourg that resulted in its capture in June 1745.

On June 6, 1746, Harrison married the very wealthy Elizabeth Pelham, Banister's youngest sister-in-law, a relative of Governor Shirley's wife and a descendant of Benedict Arnold, Rhode Island's first governor under the charter of 1663. The couple took up residence on a farm at Brenton's Cove. This union allowed Harrison the time and money for travel to

Peter Harrison, America's premier eighteenth-century architect, has left several surviving monuments to his talents in Newport, including the Redwood Library, the Brick Market and Touro Synagogue. This portrait is a copy of an original 1756 painting attributed to Nathaniel Smibert.

architecturally significant European sites and to develop an imposing architectural library.

After designing a splendid mansion in Roxbury, Massachusetts, for his new patron, Governor Shirley, Harrison produced his first public building—Newport's Redwood Library—in 1748. This skilled practitioner progressed to design King's Chapel, Boston (1749–54); the Brick Market, Newport (1761); Christ Church, Cambridge (1761); and Touro Synagogue, Newport (1762–63). In the derivation of these designs, Harrison depended on the engraved European architectural books that codified the best designs available, but he never copied buildings directly from books, for he had the talent and self-confidence to improve on what he found. To a degree, Harrison introduced to America a style of academic classicism that was influenced by the English Palladian revival. Inspired by the Italian Renaissance architect Andrea Palladio, this form of architecture was characterized by columns and porticos resembling the Greek and Roman temples of the Classical age. Amazingly, most of Harrison's work was performed without compensation. Architectural historian Fiske Kimball rates Harrison as "the most notable architect of colonial America."

The Stabilizers

In 1761, the Harrison brothers moved from Newport to New Haven, where Peter was made collector of customs in 1768 as a successor to his brother Joseph. His Anglicanism and his Loyalist sympathies subjected him to great pressure, and immediately after he died in that town seven years later, a rioting rebel mob destroyed most of his personal property, including his fine library and nearly all of his architectural drawings and papers.

The career of this remarkable, mostly self-taught gentleman-architect is described in detail by Carl Bridenbaugh, the foremost historian of urban life in colonial America, in a biography aptly entitled *Peter Harrison: First American Architect* (1949). Antoinette Downing and Vincent Scully Jr., in their classic work *The Architectural Heritage of Newport, Rhode Island* (revised edition 1967), refer to the mid-eighteenth century as "Peter Harrison's Era." According to these authorities, it was because of Harrison's "ability to adapt and interpret two-dimensional English drawings into three-dimensional colonial reality that Newport's public buildings of the years after 1748 rank among the most advanced and academic in style in the colonies."

"Most of the evidence for Harrison's career has to be circumstantial and stylistic, and hence controversial," states John Millar, one of the most learned students of Harrison's work. Millar attributes to Harrison many more than the dozen and a half designs that are fully documented, asserting the controversial claim that Harrison's output, directly and indirectly, accounted for "over 200 buildings (including more than 30 churches and more than 30 other public buildings)."

JOHN GODDARD

John Goddard, one of the most famous and skilled Newport cabinetmakers of the eighteenth century, was born in Dartmouth, Massachusetts, in 1723, the son of shipwright and housewright Daniel Goddard and Mary Tripp. Shortly after his birth, the Goddard family moved to Newport, where young John became apprenticed to cabinetmaker Job Townsend Sr. in the early 1740s. In 1746, he married his master's daughter Hannah, thus bonding the renowned Goddard-Townsend Rhode Island group of joiners and furniture makers. This connection was reinforced when John's brother James, also a cabinetmaker, married Susanna Townsend, Hannah's sister.

This secretary (desk and bookcase), originally owned by Providence civic leader John Brown, is believed to have been crafted by John Goddard, probably in the 1760s. It is now in the John Brown House Museum at 86 Power Street, Providence, a building designed by Joseph Brown that is part of the Rhode Island Historical Society.

Goddard is known mainly by his work, for relatively little is known of his personal life. He built his house and small shop on Easton's Point in 1748, held a few minor town offices during his career, including viewer of lumber, and belonged to the Quaker faith.

Goddard's clientele included many of Rhode Island's political and cultural elite, but his work did not buy him wealth. When the British occupied Newport in December 1776, Goddard moved briefly to Providence, where he opened a sales warehouse on a wharf owned by his client Moses Brown.

The Stabilizers

Goddard's business was hurt severely by dislocation and war. He returned to Newport after the conflict and died there insolvent in 1785, leaving his shop and tools to his woodworking sons—Townsend, Stephen and Thomas. According to one genealogical account, John and Hannah had a total of sixteen children.

Goddard is best known for his walnut and mahogany furniture, especially block-front, shell-carved secretaries; high chests of drawers with ball-and-claw feet; tables; and chairs. Unlike his most notable contemporary, John Townsend, he did not sign or label most of his work, and only a few documented pieces are known to exist. Among these are two secretaries (desks with bookcases on top) at the Museum of the Rhode Island School of Design. One of these secretaries is inscribed "Made by John Goddard 1761 and repaired by Thomas Goddard, his son, 1813." His famous six-shell desk/bookcase made for Providence merchant Nicholas Brown was sold in 1989 for $12.1 million—a record for a piece of American furniture at auction and an ironic twist of fate for a craftsman who died impoverished.

JOHN TOWNSEND

John Townsend (1733–1809) was one of at least nineteen family members in an extended three-generation Quaker family of Townsends and Goddards who crafted the famed Newport style of American furniture from 1740 to 1840. Newport was the destination of many cargoes of fine mahogany woods from Honduras and Santo Domingo. Wealth created by Caribbean shipping made it possible for Jewish and Quaker merchants to own fine homes and furnish them with desks, tables, chairs and clock cases, all crafted and carved in a distinctive Townsend-Goddard style, emblazoned with shell carvings reflective of Newport's maritime and oceanic heritage.

John Townsend was born in Newport in 1733, the fourth child of Christopher Townsend Sr. and Patience Easton, a descendant of one of Newport's founders. Job Townsend Sr. was his uncle, and Hannah Townsend, wife of John Goddard, was his cousin. Townsend served as an apprentice to his father in the art of cabinetmaking and opened his own shop when he was about twenty years old. His first notable piece was a dining table crafted in 1756. Active in civic affairs, he served for a period as Newport's town treasurer and as its surveyor of highways. In 1767, he married Philadelphia

Newport's Whitehorne House contains these mahogany chairs made by John Townsend (ca. 1760) and a mahogany block-and-shell chest-on-chest attributed to the Goddard-Townsend group of craftsmen. The identifying characteristics of this school of artisans were the block front and shell designs used on many of their creations. This photo is courtesy of the Newport Restoration Foundation.

Feke, the daughter of Robert Feke, America's first important native-born portrait painter.

Townsend's work was interrupted by the British occupation of Newport from December 1776 to October 1779; in 1777, he was briefly confined to a prison ship in Newport Harbor. After the war, his output of furniture was prolific, so he expanded his shop to include six parcels of land at Easton's Point in the northwest part of Newport along the waterfront. He appears to have been the most financially successful member of his clan, and he left a substantial estate at the time of his death in 1809.

According to furniture historian Gerald W.R. Ward, Townsend's furniture was made in the Newport version of the English baroque and rococo styles from approximately 1756 until the mid-1790s and then in the neoclassical style until Townsend's death. "Of consistently high quality," states Ward, "Townsend's pre-neoclassical cabinetwork represents a distinct American design statement that is bold and sculptural and that in its baroque simplicity and strength stands apart from the more heavily ornamental, asymmetrical English rococo taste... Townsend and his fellow craftsmen in Newport thus created a style of cabinetmaking that constitutes an American contribution to the history of design." Appropriately, their finely crafted works have found their way into the greatest private collections and major public museums of this country. Many Townsend-Goddard pieces have graced the halls and reception rooms of the U.S. State Department in Washington, where the best of America is on view to impress the diplomats of the world. Unlike John Goddard, however, John Townsend signed or dated some thirty-five elegant pieces between 1756 and 1800, ensuring that his fine craftsmanship would be not only prized but also recognized.

PART III

𝒯𝒽𝑒 𝓡𝑒𝓋𝑜𝓁𝓊𝓉𝒾𝑜𝓃𝒶𝓇𝒾𝑒𝓈

1763–1790

SARAH UPDIKE GODDARD

There are certain ingredients necessary to create an independent, self-governing, stable commonwealth. A thriving economy always helps. Strong, healthy community institutions like religious congregations and schools and colleges help, as do economic engines like banks and insurance societies. But a vital key to unlocking the participation of the public is the role of the press. Just as banks circulate money, the press circulates ideas. Ideas are the currency of the mind.

By the middle decades of the eighteenth century, there were a lot of ideas in Rhode Island relating to trade and government. Rhode Island's relationship to England raised questions of home rule, but these were also questions of who would rule at home.

For nearly half a century, political leadership and power had centered in Newport on a clique of powerful merchants and their offspring who had migrated to South County, where they elected representatives in league with the island towns of Aquidneck and Conanicut (Jamestown). Now, under the leadership of Stephen Hopkins, Nicholas Cooke and the Browns, Providence was beginning to challenge the domination of Newport and its ideas on how to run Rhode Island. Central to their efforts to persuade the freemen of Rhode Island—the male property owners who were eligible to make

Vox Populi, Vox Dei.
A PROVIDENCE GAZETTE
Extraordinary.

decisions in town meetings—was the creation of a Providence newspaper. Interestingly enough, the ally of the emergent Providence politicos was someone who could not vote because she was a woman: Sarah Updike Goddard (1700–1770).

Sarah Updike was born to wealth at Cocumscussoc plantation at the turn of the eighteenth century, the daughter of Ludowick and Abigail Newton Updike. Her great-grandfather was Richard Smith, a friend and associate of Roger Williams. Her education, in the fashion of the day, was by a tutor who lived in her home and also instructed her four sisters and her brother, Daniel, who would serve as Rhode Island's attorney general for a total of twenty-five years.

In 1735, Sarah married Dr. Giles Goddard of New London. Two of their four children survived into adulthood. After Dr. Goddard died of gout in 1757, their son, William, who had been an apprentice printer in New Haven and New York, set up a print

Before they resorted to the sword, American colonists took up the pen to resist what they perceived to be violations of their rights as Englishmen. Sarah Updike Goddard, editor of the *Providence Gazette*, was among the earliest dissenters. On August 24, 1765, she published this special edition of her newspaper to incite popular resistance to the Stamp Act.

shop in Providence with his mother's financial assistance, and on October 20, 1762, he began printing the *Providence Gazette and Country Journal*, the town's first newspaper. He suspended publication in the spring of 1765 and left the shop to be run by his mother and sister, Mary Katherine.

The suspension of the *Gazette* coincided with the Stamp Act crisis, so on August 24, 1765, the *Gazette* appeared again under the auspices of Sarah Goddard, who devoted a special issue to the Stamp Act, one of the defining factors at the basis of the American Revolutionary movement. Although William Goddard returned briefly in 1766, he once again departed, leaving the press in the hands of his mother and sister, who continued to print the *Providence Gazette* on a weekly basis, providing Providence with a public forum that helped to further the cause of American independence and the political career of Stephen Hopkins. In September 1767, Sarah Goddard took on John Carter as a partner, and a year later she sold the shop to Carter. She then moved to join her son in Philadelphia, where fourteen months later this pioneering printer and journalist died on January 5, 1770.

An anonymous letter appearing in the *New York Gazette* on January 22, 1770, and reprinted by her successor, John Carter, on February 11 suffices for her epitaph. It concludes with the following sentiments:

> *Her uncommon attainments in literature were the least valuable parts of her character. Her conduct through all the changing trying scenes of life, was not only unblameable, but even exemplary—a sincere piety, an unaffected humility, an easy agreeable cheerfulness and affability, an entertaining, sensible and edifying conversation, and a prudent attention to all the duties of domestic life, endeared her to all her acquaintances, especially in the relations of wife, parent, friend and neighbor. The death of such a person is a public loss, an irreparable one to her children.*

Those children honored her memory by excelling in the fields of journalism and printing. William became editor of the large and prominent *Pennsylvania Chronicle* and the *Maryland Journal*. Each newspaper, in turn, had the largest circulation in the new nation. In addition, he was a founder of the American postal system. Daughter Mary Katherine (1738–1816) was a noted printer, newspaper publisher, bookseller and postmaster in Pennsylvania and Maryland whose credits included the *Pennsylvania Chronicle*, the *Maryland Journal* and a highly regarded print shop.

SILAS DOWNER

Silas Downer (1729–1785), Patriot and lawyer, was born in Norwich, Connecticut, to a farm family that subsequently moved to Sunderland, Massachusetts, near Deerfield, where Downer got his early schooling. He entered Harvard College at age fourteen and earned an undergraduate degree and a master of arts degree by age twenty-one. After graduation in 1750, Downer came to Rhode Island to apply his remarkable talent in calligraphy as a scrivener, or professional penman, and as a copyist, letter writer and public notary. As one of the few highly educated men in the colony at that time, he soon entered into the practice of law. Among his most influential clients, who were increasingly numbered among his best friends and patrons, were Stephen and Esek Hopkins and the Brown brothers of Providence.

During the decade of the 1760s, Downer served as clerk of the upper house of the General Assembly and as librarian of the Providence Library. He also initiated the drive to build the Market House in Providence and served on a legislative committee that revised the general laws.

As the constitutional dispute with the mother country developed after 1763, Downer used his writing skills to compose a series of essays and remonstrances against the current commercial and administrative policies of England. Several of these protests have been discovered, collected and edited by Brown University historian Carl Bridenbaugh under the title *Silas Downer: Forgotten Patriot* (1974).

Downer's most important patriotic treatise was his 1768 *Discourse*, delivered at the dedication of the Liberty Tree in Providence, wherein he stated that parliamentary statutes pertaining to the governance of the colonies were "infractions on the natural rights of men" and therefore void. This work, repudiating Parliament's recently passed Declaratory Act of 1766, has been cited as the first significant challenge both to the authority of Parliament to

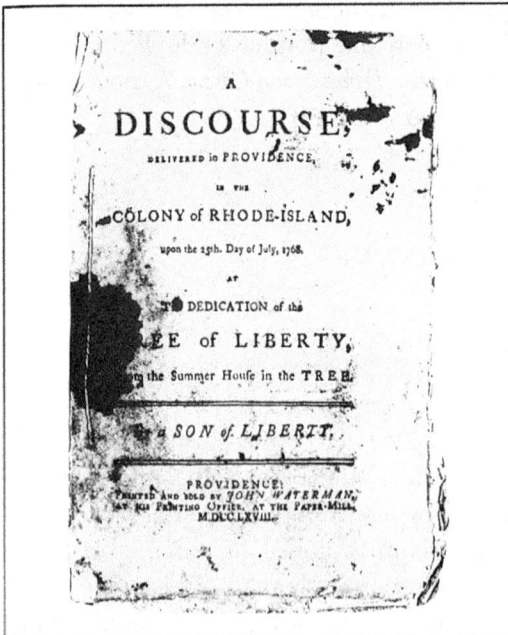

Attorney Silas Downer was Rhode Island's penman of the Revolution. Shown here is the title page of a pamphlet, which Downer published as a "Son of Liberty," containing his July 1768 discourse denouncing the Declaratory Act and the Townsend Acts. Downer and his colleague Stephen Hopkins articulated theories of empire that divided sovereignty between the colonies and the mother country.

make laws of all kinds to regulate the colonies and to the Declaratory Act's statement of undivided sovereignty in a unitary empire.

The writings of Downer's more famous colleague, Stephen Hopkins, suggested a federal theory of empire in which sovereignty was divided between the mother country, which exercised it on imperial issues, and the colonies, which exercised it over their purely local affairs. Eventually, this theory was incorporated into the Constitution of the United States to establish the relationship between the federal government and the individual states.

Actually, Downer's rhetoric carried him beyond federalism to an embryonic theory of dominion or commonwealth, wherein the American colonies gave allegiance to the sovereign while insisting on self-government. He believed that "our distant situation from Great Britain and other attendant circumstances made it impossible for us to be represented in the parliament of that country, or to be governed from thence." If this denial of parliamentary power had been officially embraced by Rhode Island (and it was not), then the colony's famed renunciation of allegiance to the king on May 4, 1776—now mistakenly celebrated as "Rhode Island Independence Day"—would have been just that. Professor Bridenbaugh (with some hyperbole) has called Downer's oration "the most important single event in the pre-revolutionary history of the colony of Rhode Island."

Downer continued his efforts as "a son of liberty," and in 1774 Stephen Hopkins took him to the First Continental Congress in Philadelphia to be secretary of the Rhode Island delegation, which was headed by Hopkins and his former rival Samuel Ward. Once war erupted, Downer served as clerk of the state's Council of War. Following the conflict, he returned to the practice of law without fanfare or notoriety. He died on December 15, 1785, at the home of his cousin in Roxbury, Massachusetts. More than any other man, Downer can be described as Rhode Island's "Penman of the Revolution."

SOLOMON SOUTHWICK

Except for those Revolutionary War Patriots who actually faced the bayonet charges or the merciless cannon fire of the British and their mercenaries, there probably were few other Rhode Islanders who put themselves and their families at more risk than "Patriot Printer" Solomon Southwick of Newport. Editor of the weekly newspaper *Newport Mercury*,

The *Newport Mercury* was outspoken in its criticism of English policy in the decade before the outbreak of hostilities. Editor Solomon Southwick, whose silhouette is shown here, did not hide in the shadows. In a town that contained some powerful Loyalists, Southwick defiantly proclaimed on the masthead of his paper the bold motto: "Undaunted by Tyrants—we'll die or be FREE!"

Southwick was a strong advocate of American independence in a town where allegiances were torn between mobs who trashed the dwelling of the local stamp tax agent of the British and those elite opinion leaders known as "the Newport Junto," who favored British rule. While most of Rhode Island's mainland took up the Patriot cause, impelled largely by the rough handling that Narragansett Bay shippers experienced from martinet British naval officers, there were a number of prominent people in Newport, Rhode Island's leading town who upheld the British cause. In fact, the six votes cast in the Rhode Island House of Deputies against the famous renunciation of allegiance of May 4, 1776, were those of the Newport delegation. To their mind, a rebellious newspaper editor who bought his ink by the barrel was an opponent whose opinion had to be silenced.

Southwick, the son of Solomon and Mary Southwick, lived in the Point section of town among the clockmakers, furniture makers and other colonial craftsmen and was a member of the influential Quaker community. He received a formal education at the College of Philadelphia (now the University of Pennsylvania). Upon his return to Newport, he secured the political backing of a prominent merchant, Henry Collins, and married the widowed daughter of Lieutenant Governor John Gardner.

In addition to his newspaper work, Southwick was also a printer of books, almanacs and pamphlets. In the years leading up to the Revolution, he enjoyed the patronage of the colony as the official printer of laws,

The Revolutionaries

and thus he became one of the local printers of the Declaration of Independence. Southwick's fealty to the American cause of independence was reflected in the masthead motto of the *Newport Mercury*: "Undaunted by Tyrants—we'll die or be FREE." The consequences of a bold challenge to British rule became imminent when the *Mercury* suspended operations, and Southwick dismantled his press and hid it just prior to the arrival of Sir Henry Clinton and his army of British and Hessian troops.

Beginning in December 1776, the British occupation of Newport lasted for nearly three years, and Southwick became a hunted man. He narrowly escaped capture, fleeing the town in an open boat with his wife and child, Solomon Jr., as a party of British regulars arrived on the shoreline. The Southwicks went first to Rehoboth, Massachusetts, and later to Attleboro, where Solomon resumed publishing the laws of Rhode Island. He was appointed deputy commissary general of issues by the Rhode Island General Assembly in 1777 and 1778.

Southwick arrived in Providence in 1779 and set up a printing office with Bennett Wheeler. This rebellious duo began to publish the *American Journal and General Advertiser* in March of that year. When the British evacuated Newport in October 1779, Southwick returned to the town and, by 1783, was back in the book publishing business. Two years later, his name appeared once again in the masthead of the *Mercury.*

The degree of public favor he enjoyed was reflected by his designation to be one of four hosts to welcome George Washington to Newport in August 1790, when the nation's first president came to acknowledge Rhode Island's belated ratification of the federal Constitution. Solomon Southwick died in 1797 and was buried at Newport's Common Burying Ground, where his memorial reads:

> *Just, generous, benevolent, and sincere...*
> *Was he whose hallowed dust reposes here;*
> *If 'er a partial prayer he breathed to heaven*
> *That prayer was for his country's glory given.*

Southwick's only son and namesake followed his father's footsteps, becoming publisher of the *Albany Register* and holder of several important political positions in New York State.

Reverend Dr. Ezra Stiles

Ezra Stiles (1727–1795) was born in North Haven, Connecticut, the son of Isaac Stiles, a Yale-educated Congregational minister, and Kezia Taylor, who died five days after his birth. Ezra entered Yale himself at age fifteen and graduated at nineteen in 1746. Three years later, he entered the ministry. As a young man, he also studied and practiced law and conducted experiments in electricity in correspondence with Benjamin Franklin.

In 1755, at the age of twenty-eight, Stiles took an assignment as minister of Newport's Second Congregational Church, where he served with distinction for over two decades. Small in stature and of "a very delicate structure," Stiles was nonetheless a first-rate preacher, described by contemporaries as "always tolerant and distressed by sectarian bickering." During his tenure in Newport, Stiles became an intellectual and civic leader. He served as librarian of the Redwood Library and, though a Congregationalist, wrote the initial draft of the charter for the Baptist-sponsored Rhode Island College (later Brown University). His draft called for mutual tolerance and religious liberty and prohibited all religious tests for either faculty or students. At various times he attended Quaker, Jewish, Dutch Reformed, Anglican and Catholic services to acquaint himself with those religions.

Stiles became a spokesman for the Patriot cause in the decade prior to the Revolution, and he left Newport in December 1776, when the British came to occupy that town. During 1777 and early 1778, he served as pastor of the Congregational church in Portsmouth, New Hampshire.

An indefatigable note taker and writer, in 1769 Stiles began a literary diary that would reach fifteen volumes by the time of his death in 1795. This record is a major source for events in pre-Revolutionary Rhode Island and for the progress of the war in New England. In addition, Stiles wrote six volumes of manuscript notes on his travels ("Itineraries") from 1760 to 1794 and a host of other papers, which he donated to the archives of Yale University.

Because of his reputation as one of the most literate and learned men in New England, Stiles was called to his alma mater, Yale, in 1778 to become its president and a professor of ecclesiastical history and Semitic languages. His knowledge of Hebrew—acquired by his intellectual interaction with Rabbi Haim Isaac Carigal, Rabbi Isaac Touro and other members of Newport's Jewish synagogue—allowed him to translate large portions of the Old Testament into English. In his later years, his sermons and writings were notable for their espousal of democracy and their opposition to slavery. Stiles engaged in an impressive variety of intellectual pursuits during his career: he was a linguist (Hebrew, Arabic, Syriac, Armenian and French), an amateur scientist (electricity, astronomy, chemistry and zoology), a theologian and an ecclesiastical historian.

Stiles married twice, first to Elizabeth Hubbard of New Haven in 1757. Of the eight children she bore him prior to her death in 1775, only five outlived their father. In 1782, he married Mary (Cranston) Checkley, a widow; the daughter of Benjamin Cranston of Newport, she was a member of one of the town's leading families.

In May 1795, at the age of sixty-seven, the still active and enormously productive Stiles contracted a fever and died within a week.

The Reverend Dr. Ezra Stiles, Newport's most learned resident, had been so outspoken in his criticism of English policy that he had to leave town in December 1776 just prior to the arrival of a British occupying force. Newport's loss was New Haven's gain. In 1778, his alma mater, Yale, recruited Stiles as its president. His posthumous portrait, painted about 1812 by Reuben Moulthrop, was presented to Newport's Redwood Library by a Stiles descendant.

His notable career is detailed in a fine biography by Edmund S. Morgan appropriately entitled *The Gentle Puritan* (1962). Though altered, the Stiles house in Newport, at 14 Clarke Street, has been preserved.

GOVERNOR AND CHIEF JUSTICE SAMUEL WARD

Samuel Ward (1725–1776) was born in Newport, one of fourteen children of Governor Richard Ward and Mary (Tillinghast) Ward. He was twice descended (in both paternal and maternal lines) from Roger Williams. His father, a prosperous merchant, served as governor of Rhode Island from 1740 to 1743. Young Sam was destined by his father to be a gentleman farmer and merchant. In 1745, he married Ann Ray, of Block Island, who would bear him five sons and six daughters. Moving to the small port town of Westerly to live on land acquired from his father-in-law, he farmed, exported produce to Newport and Boston and grew wealthy.

Ward's election in 1756 as a deputy to the General Assembly from Westerly marked the beginning of his public service and the escalation of a political feud between Ward's faction, led by Newport merchants and South County planters, and a faction centered in Providence and supported by other northern towns, led by Stephen Hopkins, Nicholas Cooke and the Brown family, who were challenging the old Newport and South County elite. The principal goal of the two factions was to secure control of the legislature in order to obtain the host of public offices at the disposal of that powerful body. In these circumstances, the governor, as a symbol and party leader, acquired an informal influence far beyond his meager constitutional power. One of the principal architects of that party system, Ward would three times win election as governor—in 1762, 1765 and 1766.

Although he lacked legal training, in 1761 Ward was chosen by the General Assembly as chief justice of the colony. In this capacity, and to his discredit, he delivered a decision against the naturalization of those professing the Jewish faith. As a devout Sabbatarian Baptist, he became one of the original trustees of Rhode Island College (now Brown University) in 1764.

Defeated in 1767 for reelection as governor, despite his bold defiance of the Stamp Act—he was the only colonial governor who refused to take the oath to enforce it—Ward retired to Westerly, and by 1770 the Hopkins forces had established their political dominance. To add to Ward's discouragement, his wife, Anna, died in 1770.

After the Boston Tea Party of 1773 and the passage by England of the so-called Intolerable Acts in early 1774, Ward again entered the public arena as an outspoken critic of British policy and as an advocate for establishing inter-colonial committees of correspondence to mobilize unified resistance to the mother country. He put aside his differences with Hopkins as both departed for Philadelphia in 1774 to serve in the Continental Congress. During the second session of that revolutionary assembly, Ward was called by John Hancock to preside over the Congress when that body resolved itself into a committee of the whole for debate and voting, and he was one of the

The Revolutionaries

Governor and Chief Justice Samuel Ward was the titular leader of a political faction based in Newport and South County that contested with a Providence-based party led by Stephen Hopkins. Both men put aside their differences in 1774 to attend the Continental Congress, where they formulated policies to resist what each regarded as British encroachments on the rights of American colonists. Ward's portrait by an unkown artist is in the possession of the Rhode Island Historical Society.

delegates to propose and secure the appointment of George Washington as commander in chief of the Continental army.

In March 1776, as the Second Continental Congress was moving toward a declaration of independence, Ward (who had refused inoculation) contracted smallpox and died. He would assuredly have joined Hopkins as a Rhode Island signer had he lived a few months longer. Instead, that duty fell to William Ellery of Newport, Ward's ally and supporter. Ward's remains lie in Newport's Common Burial Ground, where he was reinterred from Philadelphia in 1860, not far from the grave of Ellery.

Among Ward's many prominent descendants were his son Lieutenant Colonel Samuel Ward II (1756–1832), a Revolutionary War hero and merchant; his grandson Samuel Ward III (1786–1839), a powerful New York banker; and a great-granddaughter, Julia Ward Howe, a women's rights advocate, the author of "The Battle Hymn of the Republic" and a summer resident of Portsmouth.

GOVERNOR, CHIEF JUSTICE AND SIGNER STEPHEN HOPKINS

Stephen Hopkins (1707–1785), statesman, pamphleteer and signer of the Declaration of Independence, was born on March 7, 1707, in Providence, easterly of a former Indian village called Mashapaug. This site was set off from Providence in 1754, becoming part of the new town of Cranston. It was reannexed in 1868 and is located today in the Elmwood section of Providence.

Hopkins—the second of nine children born to farmers William Hopkins Jr. (ca. 1681–1738) and Ruth Wilkinson (b. 1686), a devout Quaker—moved at an early age with his parents and older brother to a farm at Chopmist, in a part of the "outlands" of Providence that were incorporated as the town of Scituate in 1731. On this agricultural frontier, Hopkins grew to manhood, working on his parents' farm and acquiring skill as a surveyor. In 1726, he married Sarah Scott (1707–1753), of Providence, who bore him seven children in a marriage that endured until her death by suicide after a debilitating illness. Five of his children lived to maturity.

Though he lacked formal education, the man John Adams would later describe as a person of "wit, humour, anecdotes, science, and learning" became the first town moderator of Scituate in 1731 at the age of twenty-four. This post was the initial step in a political career that included election to the office of Speaker of the Rhode Island House of Representatives (seven times), service as governor (nine one-year terms), appointment to the position of chief justice of Rhode Island's highest court (eleven years) and

The Revolutionaries

Governor, chief justice and signer Stephen Hopkins was not only one of two Rhode Islanders to affix his name to the Declaration of Independence, but he also headed all three branches of Rhode Island's government, serving terms as governor, chief justice and Speaker of the House. This preliminary sketch by artist John Trumbull was done in 1791, six years after Hopkins's death, using Rufus Hopkins to model for his dead father—whom, it was said, he strongly resembled.

selection as a Rhode Island delegate to the First and Second Continental Congresses (1774–79).

The rise of Hopkins in the world of government was accompanied by his rapid ascent in the business of trade and commerce. Having moved in 1742 from rural Scituate, which he represented in the state legislature, to the port town of Providence, where he immediately secured reelection to the General Assembly and resumed the post of House Speaker, which he first held in 1738, Hopkins formed business partnerships with prominent Newport merchant Godfrey Malbone and then with the powerful Brown family, Providence's leading eighteenth-century entrepreneurs. Thereafter, his wealth and financial connections fueled his rise to political prominence.

Hopkins's first significant foray into inter-colonial politics came in 1754, when he represented Rhode Island at the Albany Congress. Farsighted enough to see the advantages of colonial cooperation and practical enough to realize the potential usefulness of a strong colonial navy in protecting commerce (one of the suggestions made by that congress), Hopkins favored the plan of union devised at Albany and wrote a pamphlet defending his participation in the locally unpopular conclave.

In 1755, Hopkins was elected to his first term as governor, a post with little constitutional power under Rhode Island's system of legislative ascendancy. Nonetheless, he began to exert considerable political strength and influence as the leader of the dominant faction in the colony's emergent two-party system—one of America's first.

In this political milieu, opposing groups—one headed by Samuel Ward of Westerly and the other by Hopkins—were organized with sectional overtones; generally speaking (though with notable exceptions), the merchants and farmers of southern Rhode Island (Ward) battled with their counterparts from Providence and its environs (Hopkins). The principal goal of these groups was to secure control of the powerful legislature in order to obtain the host of public offices—from chief justice to inspector of tobacco—at the disposal of that body.

The semi-permanent nature, relatively stable membership and explicit sectional rivalry of the warring camps have led historian Mack Thompson to describe Rhode Island's pre-Revolutionary political structure as one of "stable factionalism." Another historian, David S. Lovejoy, has boldly maintained that Rhode Islanders revolted from British rule not only "on the broad grounds of constitutional right to keep Rhode Island safe for liberty and property" but also to preserve "the benefits of party politics"—patronage and spoils.

Rampant factionalism, with Hopkins usually prevailing, endured until 1768, when Ward and Hopkins agreed to retire from future gubernatorial races. A now humorous incident in this political war occurred in March 1757, when the Hopkins-controlled legislature set off a forty-four-square-mile town from the northern part of Sam Ward's Westerly and named the new municipality "Hopkinton." In 1770, Hopkins again became chief justice, an office he first held in 1751. He continued to hold this top judicial post for another six years, even after he and his former rival, Ward, went to Philadelphia in 1774 to represent Rhode Island's interests in the First Continental Congress.

When England began to reorganize its American empire in 1763 at the conclusion of the Seven Years' War, Hopkins set about developing and articulating economic and political proposals that ran counter to parliamentary enactments. In the radical *Providence Gazette*, which he helped to establish in 1762, Hopkins opposed the renewal of the Molasses Act upon its expiration in 1764. He denounced the measure's six-pence-per-gallon duty on foreign molasses as destructive of Rhode Island's lucrative triangular trade with Africa and the West Indies and a levy that diminished Rhode Island's ability to buy British manufactures or pay British creditors. The Sugar Act of 1764 reduced the duty to three pence, but that toll was far greater than the 0.5 percent duty recommended by Hopkins in his essay, and the new levy was marked by much more vigorous enforcement than the old.

Late in 1764, Hopkins penned a more elaborate analysis of imperial relations, one that shifted from a purely economical defense of colonial rights to a political and constitutional conception of the British Empire. In this pamphlet, *The Rights of Colonies Examined*, Hopkins repeatedly referred not merely to the economic interests of Rhode Islanders or of the northern colonists (as in his earlier essay) but rather to the broad rights of "Americans." This treatise is notable in that it suggests a federal theory of empire, with Parliament legislating on matters of imperial concern—war, trade, international relations—but with colonial assemblies possessing sovereignty in local affairs, including taxation. In 1766, this bold tract was published in London under the title *The Grievances of the American Colonists Candidly Examined*.

In 1768, another Providence lawyer, Silas Downer—a colleague, friend and protégé of Hopkins—delivered a path-breaking public discourse at the local "Liberty Tree," repudiating the recently passed Declaratory Act and denying the authority of Parliament to make any laws of any kind to regulate the colonies. In 1774, Hopkins took attorney Downer to the First Continental Congress to serve as secretary to the Rhode Island delegation, which was headed by Hopkins and his former rival, Samuel Ward.

Influenced by his Quaker beliefs and his own professions of liberty, Hopkins freed his slaves in 1773, and the following year, while serving in the state legislature, he cosponsored a statute that prohibited the importation of "Negroes" to Rhode Island, proclaiming in its preamble:

> *Whereas, the inhabitants of America are generally engaged in the preservation of their own rights and liberties, among which, that of personal freedom must be considered as the greatest; those who are desirous of enjoying all the advantages of liberty themselves, should be willing to extend personal liberty to others.*

During the Second Continental Congress, which convened in September 1775, Hopkins became chairman of the naval committee, and he secured for his brother Esek (1718–1802) the position of first commodore and commander in chief of the newly created Continental navy. Then, as chairman of the naval and marine committee, Stephen supervised the civilian administration of the American navy.

In July 1776, Hopkins became one of two Rhode Island signers of the Declaration of Independence (William Ellery was the other). When he affixed his signature to the engrossed copy of this momentous document on August 2, 1776, he guided his palsied right hand with his left, allegedly remarking, "My hand trembles, but my heart does not." During this pivotal year, Hopkins also served as the Rhode Island member of the thirteen-man committee that drafted the Articles of Confederation, America's first written constitution

Declining health, including what was then described as "shaking palsy," limited Hopkins's role in the events of the Revolution. Despite his election as delegate, he was unable to attend sessions of Congress in Philadelphia after 1776, but he did serve from December 1776 to May 1778 on the Rhode Island Council of War, an ad hoc body established by the legislature to supervise and direct Rhode Island's war effort. In addition, he was a delegate to the convention of New England states in 1776, 1777 and 1779, serving as the convention's president in 1777.

In his declining years, Hopkins continued his productive relationship with the powerful and versatile Brown family of Providence, to whom he was bound by ties of family, religion, literary and civic projects and commercial enterprise. In 1781, he had an unexpected visit from George Washington, who had come to Rhode Island to consult with Count Rochambeau, then quartered with his French army in Newport. Houseguest Moses Brown (who, like Hopkins, was a leading Quaker businessman) remarked on the "unaffected friendliness" of the two revolutionaries as they talked about the war and the upcoming Virginia campaign. In January 1782, Ann Smith, his second wife of twenty-seven years, died. By that time, five of Hopkins's seven children (all by his first marriage) had also predeceased him.

On July 13, 1785, Hopkins—governor, jurist, legislator, Patriot, pamphleteer, farmer, merchant, educator (he was the first chancellor of Brown University), amateur scientist and civic leader—died peacefully in his Providence home, a structure now preserved as a national historic site, and was buried at Providence's North Burial Ground.

Captain Abraham Whipple

Abraham Whipple (1733–1819) was a successful privateer and naval officer who was born in Providence, the son of Noah and Mary Whipple. Of humble origins, Whipple went to sea at an early age and became associated with the wealthy and influential Brown family of merchant entrepreneurs. During the French and Indian War, he served as a privateersman under the command of Esek Hopkins and then captained his own vessel, the *Gamecock*, which captured twenty-three French vessels in 1759–60. In 1761, Whipple enhanced his status by marrying Hopkins's daughter, Sarah, who bore him three children.

In June 1772, Whipple and John Brown led a party of Rhode Islanders in the scandalous and successful foray down Narragansett Bay to burn the English revenue schooner *Gaspee*, commanded by Lieutenant William Dudingston, which had run aground on Warwick's Namquid Point while recklessly chasing the smaller packet ship *Hannah*, under the command of Captain Benjamin Lindsay. Lindsay docked in Providence, where news of the incident spread quickly. Led by merchant John Brown, that evening the townsmen assembled in Sabin's Tavern to plot the destruction of the *Gaspee*. The rebels embarked from Fenner's Wharf in eight five-oared longboats under Whipple's command. After midnight, the attack party reached the stranded ship, and following an exchange of shouts, James Bucklin shot and wounded Lieutenant Dudingston in the groin. The Providence men thereupon boarded the *Gaspee*, overpowered the crew and burned the sloop and its contents. The incident sparked an exchange of notes between Whipple and Captain James Wallace, the

In this U.S. Naval Academy portrait by Edward Savage, Captain Abraham Whipple looks rather foppish and out of character for the man who served as a privateersman, led the *Gaspee* raiders and cut out eleven prizes from England's sixty-ship Jamaica fleet.

commander of the HMS *Rose*, the flagship of the British squadron that patrolled Narragansett Bay to apprehend colonial smugglers. "You Abraham Whipple on 10 June 1772 burned his majesty's vessel the *Gaspee*, and I will hang you at the yardarm!" Wallace wrote, to which Whipple defiantly replied, "Sir, always catch a man before you hang him."

A royal investigation of the burning yielded insufficient evidence to indict the perpetrators, who were shielded by their fellow townsmen despite a reward of up to £1,000 offered by King George himself for information leading to the conviction of the *Gaspee* raiders. But the *Gaspee* inquiry led to the establishment by rebels of legislative committees of correspondence throughout the colonies—a major step on the road to the Revolution.

Whipple's experience and reputation as a seaman and Patriot made him the logical choice to command the two-vessel Rhode Island navy when it was formed by the General Assembly in June 1775. His Rhode Island flagship, the sloop *Katy*, was then taken into the Continental navy and renamed *Providence*, with Whipple still in command. Later, Whipple was given another ship, the *Columbus*, and joined his father-in-law, Esek Hopkins, in the American attack on the Bahamas in March 1776.

In 1778, Whipple took command of a new frigate, also called *Providence*, and outrunning the British blockade of Narragansett Bay, he made a successful voyage to France to deliver dispatches and to obtain valuable supplies of arms and uniforms. Whipple's most famous wartime exploit occurred in July 1779, when the *Providence* was cruising in company with the *Queen of France* and the *Ranger* off the coast of Newfoundland. Early on the morning of July 18, through heavy fog, the Americans heard the sound of ship bells. Whipple soon realized that he had sailed into Britain's Jamaica fleet, consisting of sixty vessels heavily laden with cargo. The three American ships ran up the British flag and then cut out eleven prizes, seven of which they brought safely to Boston, where they were sold at auction. It was the richest haul of the Revolution, and with the proceeds divided between the captors and Congress, Whipple and his crew shared nearly $1 million.

In December 1779, toward the end of the war, Whipple was sent to Charleston, South Carolina, to help defend it against British attack, and when the city fell on May 12, 1780, he was taken prisoner. Later released on parole for the duration of the war, he never resumed his duties as a naval officer, but as a master in 1784, he sailed the first American flag vessel, the *George Washington*, into the River Thames in England. Whipple left Rhode Island in 1788 and headed west with James Mitchell Varnum to the Northwest Territory, where he settled on a farm in Marietta, Ohio, with his family. Aside from a spectacular voyage down the Ohio and Mississippi Rivers to New Orleans and Havana in 1801, Whipple lived uneventfully in Marietta, dying there in 1819. He is buried, along with Varnum, at Marietta's Mound Cemetery. The U.S. Navy has since honored him by naming three ships in his memory and by displaying his full-size portrait at the U.S. Naval Academy at Annapolis.

COMMODORE ESEK HOPKINS

Esek Hopkins (1718–1802) was one of nine children born in Scituate to farmers William Hopkins Jr. and Ruth Wilkinson. His older brother and patron was governor and signer Stephen Hopkins. Upon the death of his father, Esek went to sea at the age of twenty and eventually served on several merchant vessels. As a sailor, he rose rapidly in command and acquired a reputation for his skill and leadership ability. In 1741, he married Desire Burroughs and moved with her to Newport, where they began a family that eventually consisted of ten children.

During the French and Indian War (1754–63), Hopkins commanded a privateer that seized several French prizes. His handsome profits allowed him to buy a substantial farm in the northern area of Providence that was soon set off as the town of North Providence in 1765, though it was reannexed in 1874. His farmhouse on Admiral Street, now owned by the City of Providence, has been preserved and is listed on the National Register of Historic Places.

During the 1760s, Hopkins continued his seafaring ways, making voyages to Africa and the West Indies as a captain for Nicholas Brown and Company. The most notable and ignominious trip was the brig *Sally*'s voyage to the west coast of Africa to trade for slaves. According to detailed records kept by Hopkins himself, the voyage was a disaster, not merely financially but also in its toll of human lives: 109 of the 196 slaves bought from African chieftains died as a result of their ordeal. There is no record that Hopkins visited Africa again, and by 1772, he had become a full-fledged farmer.

In April 1775, the month of the Battles at Lexington and Concord, Esek Hopkins was called into service for the rebel cause, first as a battery commander and then as a brigadier general commanding his state's military defenses. Meanwhile, his powerful brother Stephen and other members

In this engraving by J.C. Buttre, Commodore Esek Hopkins appears taciturn and benign. He was neither. The first commander in chief of the U.S. Navy was forceful, strong-willed and intolerant of criticism. The last-mentioned trait cost him his job in early 1778, so he became a Rhode Island state legislator and a member of the Rhode Island Council of War for the duration of the conflict with England.

The Revolutionaries

of the Continental Congress were working in Philadelphia to establish an American navy.

In the final months of 1775, Congress assembled a manned fleet of eight vessels, the first of which were the sloop *Providence* (formerly John Brown's *Katy*) and the *Alfred*. Rhode Island delegate Stephen Hopkins, a leader in this effort, persuaded Congress to appoint his brother, Esek, as the embryonic navy's commander in chief with the title of commodore. On January 5, 1776, Hopkins received orders to use his small squadron to clear marauding British warships from Chesapeake Bay and the Carolina coast. In the reasonable belief that the larger British vessels were too formidable to attack, Hopkins relied on the discretion granted in his instructions and sailed instead for a British base in the Bahamas, where he landed at New Providence on March 3 with a force of 270 men. This successful foray, which captured Forts Nassau and Montagu and seized a large number of cannons and munitions, is regarded as the first amphibious assault by the U.S. Marines.

After this initial success and the capture of three small British warships on the return trip to Rhode Island, it was all downhill for Commodore Hopkins. His fleet encountered the British frigate *Glasgow* off Block Island, and in the ensuing battle, the larger British ship outmaneuvered the American force, inflicting heavy damage before its successful escape.

John Hancock of Massachusetts, the president of the Continental Congress, complimented Hopkins at the conclusion of this Bahama mission: "I beg leave to congratulate you on the success of your expedition. Your account of the spirit and bravery shown by the men affords them [Congress] the greatest satisfaction." Notwithstanding Hancock's praise and that of John Adams and William Ellery, Congress's southern delegates were already angry with Hopkins because of his decision not to engage the British ships along their coastline. When news of the embarrassing encounter with the *Glasgow* arrived in Philadelphia, Hopkins was summoned to that city to defend his conduct. Having been a shipmaster and commander for three decades, he was imperious, assertive and intolerant of criticism. This demeanor contributed to his censure by Congress on August 16, 1776, but he retained his command.

Hopkins worked to prepare his vessels for action when he returned to Rhode Island waters, but he faced recruitment problems and delays when many sailors opted for more lucrative duty aboard privateers. Then, in December 1776, a large British force began the occupation of Newport, thereby preventing Hopkins and his ships from leaving Narragansett Bay.

The frustrated commodore was further criticized by southern congressmen and by many of his own officers, and he boldly returned the criticism. His insubordination to Congress resulted first in his suspension and then in a vote in January 1778 that he be "dismissed from the service of the United States." By that date, his brother, Stephen, had left Philadelphia because of ill health.

Together with his strong supporter, John Adams, Hopkins believed that he was a victim of sectional animosity. He was so embittered by his dismissal that he never commanded another vessel. However, he did not retire from public life. He served in the state's General Assembly from 1777 to 1786, he held the post of collector of imposts (tariffs) for Rhode Island in 1783 and he was a trustee of Rhode Island College (Brown University) from 1782 until his death in February 1802.

Esek's son, John B. Hopkins (1742–1796), a *Gaspee* raider, did his part to refurbish his family's seafaring reputation. He commanded the Rhode Island–built frigate *Warren*, the flagship of a small squadron that captured seven British merchant ships and one warship during 1779.

COLONEL CHRISTOPHER GREENE

Christopher Greene (1737–1781) of Warwick, a direct descendant of Roger Williams and the second son of Judge Phillip and Elizabeth Wickes Greene, was one of Rhode Island's most illustrious military figures of the American Revolution.

Prior to the outbreak of war, Greene married Ann Lippitt, by whom he had nine children, and he engaged in economic activities in the Pawtuxet Valley that included a partnership in the operation of forges and sawmills. He also served as a deputy from Warwick in the state legislature. Christopher was a third cousin of Nathanael Greene, with whom he had a business relationship.

Tall and powerfully built, Greene was an inspiring leader who held positions of command from the outset of the conflict, commencing with the post of lieutenant in the Kentish Guards, a local militia group founded in 1774. He led a battalion of troops in Benedict Arnold's ill-fated 1775 expedition to seize Quebec, moving with the forces that went by boat up the Kennebec River and then marched through the woods to Quebec City. When the American assault failed in December 1775, Greene was captured

The Revolutionaries

This portrait of Colonel Christopher Greene was executed by James Sullivan Lincoln, the noted nineteenth-century Rhode Island portraitist, from an unsigned original owned by Brown University. This courageous and daring commander of Rhode Island's famed Black Regiment met his death in New York when he was ambushed by a Tory force on May 14, 1781.

and held until a prisoner exchange in August 1777. He then returned to active combat.

In October 1777, Greene made a stalwart defense of Fort Mercer at Red Bank, New Jersey, one of the forts constructed by the rebels along the

Delaware River to guard the eastern approaches to Philadelphia. Greene held this installation with 400 men against an attacking force of 1,200 professional Hessian troops. When asked to surrender prior to battle, Greene allegedly replied to the Hessian commander, Count Carl von Donop, "With these brave fellows this fort will be my tomb." When the Hessians attacked, Greene retreated to the inner walls, from which his troops subjected the attackers to withering fire. When the shooting stopped, 153 Hessians were dead and over 200 were wounded—some mortally, including Donop. The American losses were 14 killed and 23 wounded.

In February 1778, the Rhode Island General Assembly chose Greene to enlist a battalion of slaves to serve as part of the First Rhode Island Regiment and bring that unit back to full strength, a proposal first advanced by Greene's former commander, General James Mitchell Varnum. This now famous statute provided that "every able-bodied Negro, mulatto, or Indian man slave" having enlisted and "passing muster before Colonel Christopher Greene be immediately discharged from the service of his master or mistress, and be absolutely FREE, as though he had never been encumbered with any kind of servitude or slavery." The act also provided for compensation to the master or mistress. The number of such men who enlisted to fight in return for their freedom is not certain; estimates vary from 130 to 181. But that they served with distinction under Greene at the Battle of Rhode Island on August 29, 1778, and in subsequent engagements is certain.

In early 1781 the First and Second Rhode Island Regiments (the entire state military force) were consolidated into one regiment because battle deaths and injuries had depleted each unit. Christopher Greene was the natural choice to command it. On May 14, 1781, at this regiment's base on the Croton River above New York City, Colonel Greene was surprised by a band of Tories and killed. The attackers then carried his body into the woods and mutilated it, a tragic end for one of Rhode Island's greatest Revolutionary warriors. A commonly advanced theory to explain such brutality was that it constituted retribution for leading black soldiers against the British Crown.

MAJOR GENERAL NATHANAEL GREENE

Nathanael Greene was born in the Potowomut section of the town of Warwick on July 27, 1742 (or August 7, according to the New Style Julian calendar adopted in England and the American colonies in 1752). His father, for whom he was named, was a farmer and an iron maker whose second wife, Mary Mott, was Nathanael's mother. Both parents were devout Quakers who did not encourage literary accomplishments and advanced learning, so young Nathanael educated himself while working at his father's forge. As an ironmonger, Greene made frequent trips to Hope Furnace in Scituate, establishing a business and a personal relationship with the furnace owners—Scituate native Stephen Hopkins and the Brown family of Providence. These contacts undoubtedly aided his later meteoric rise in the military service.

In 1770, Greene moved to Coventry, just before his father's death, to take charge of the family forge in that town. Meanwhile, he continued his studies in law, politics, mathematics and, especially, military strategy and tactics. Eventually, he would develop a personal library on these subjects that exceeded two hundred volumes.

This militant Quaker greatly enhanced his political (and military) fortunes in 1774 by marrying Catharine Littlefield ("Caty"), a member of a leading Block Island family. At the time of the wedding of the thirty-two-year-old businessman to the vivacious nineteen-year-old Caty, the bride was living in East Greenwich with the aunt for whom she was named and her aunt's husband, William Greene—future House Speaker and then Rhode Island governor (1778–86) and member of the Council of War. Another of Caty's aunts, Ann Ray, was married to former governor Samuel Ward of Westerly, who befriended Greene and corresponded with him. In business and by marriage, Nathanael had bridged the famous Ward-Hopkins political divide. So, too, did these former antagonists, who in 1774 joined hands as the Rhode Island delegates to the First Continental Congress.

Some accounts of Greene's life assert that he was elected in 1770, 1771, 1772 and 1775 as a deputy from Coventry to the General Assembly. In-depth research by Richard Showman and Robert McCarthy, editors of the thirteen-volume *Papers of General Nathanael Greene*, persuasively contend that another Coventry man with the identical name was the state legislator. The future general had powerful legislative allies but never served in the Rhode Island General Assembly.

Rumors of resistance to British rule and such local acts of defiance as the burning of the English revenue ship *Gaspee* in June 1772 had already mobilized Greene to action. He was expelled from the Quakers in 1773 for his martial spirit, and in 1774 he served on a legislative committee to revise the colony's militia laws and to plan for the defense of Rhode Island against British invasion. In that eventful year, he was also a prime mover in the creation of an East Greenwich militia company that became the Kentish Guards. When he was rejected as an officer in this unit because of a limp caused by a childhood injury, he volunteered as a private. Realizing the ridiculousness of this situation, on May 8, 1775, Nathanael's friends in the General Assembly commissioned him a brigadier general in the fifteen-hundred-man "army of observation" that it created on April 25, 1775, a week after the skirmishes at Lexington and Concord. Perhaps never in the annals of American military history did a man experience such a rapid rise in rank from private to general.

Greene promptly reported with his army to General George Washington to join in the siege of Boston. Washington, the newly installed commander in chief of the Continental army (appointed to his top post with critical support from New Englanders such as Sam Ward and Stephen Hopkins), promptly gave Greene the rank of brigadier general in the Continental army on June 22, 1775.

Greene's first military venture ended well for the Americans when the British evacuated Boston on March 17, 1776—an event that gave future generations the opportunity to create a state holiday that honored both Washington and St. Patrick. At Boston, Greene won the friendship and earned the respect of Washington, who marked the Rhode Islander for future high responsibility in the Continental army. While conducting the siege, Greene wrote several times to Congressman Sam Ward. "Permit me then," he wrote on one occasion, "to recommend from the sincerity of my heart, ready at all times to bleed in my country's cause, a Declaration of Independence, and call upon the world and the Great God who governs it to witness the necessity, propriety, and rectitude thereof"—sentiments amazingly anticipatory of Jefferson and his actual declaration.

In 1776, Greene moved to the New York theatre of war, where his performance was as undistinguished as American operations there. Partially because of his decision not to evacuate Fort Washington on Manhattan when it became endangered, the British captured the fort and took twenty-eight hundred American prisoners. He was then given command of Forts Washington and Lee on the New Jersey side of the Hudson north of New York City, but he relinquished them to General William Howe's superior force. Fortunately, Washington (who shared in these setbacks) retained confidence in Greene's military knowledge and ability and in his ardent dedication to the cause of independence, and Greene was promoted to the rank of major general in August 1776. In the retreat of the Continentals

The Revolutionaries

Major General Nathanael Greene has been described as "Rhode Island's most notable contribution to the Revolutionary War effort." Many military historians feel that Greene was America's most skillful practitioner of what we now call "guerrilla warfare," a tactic he used in his brilliant southern campaign of 1780–81 against General Charles Cornwallis. This portrait was painted by noted Philadelphia artist Charles Willson Peale.

across New Jersey, "the cockpit of the Revolution," Greene vindicated Washington's confidence in him, especially in developing the plan for the successful attack on Trenton, in thwarting Howe's maneuver against Washington's right flank at Brandywine and in his penetrations of enemy lines at Germantown, followed by a masterful retreat to safety.

Greene spent the winter of 1777–78 at Valley Forge with Washington, an experience that impressed on Congress America's dire need to feed, clothe, equip and supply its fighting men. Accordingly, both Congress and Washington pressured the reluctant Greene to assume the vital and thankless post of quartermaster general. Greene accepted, but on the condition that he not be relieved of battlefield command. During the next two years, he vastly improved the flow of supplies to the troops in the field, but the thanks he received from some quarters was counteracted by baseless charges of war profiteering. Actually, Greene often expended his own funds or his own credit during the course of the conflict and left the army in 1783 heavily in debt.

During his stint as quartermaster, Greene managed to excel in the American victories at Monmouth and Springfield, New Jersey, and in the August 29, 1778 American victory in the one-day Battle of Rhode Island. Here he joined with fellow Rhode Islanders General James Mitchell Varnum, Colonel Christopher Greene, Major Sam Ward Jr., Captains Silas Talbot and Stephen Olney and the Black Regiment—all under the command of General John Sullivan—to decisively repulse a determined British-Hessian effort to disrupt the American withdrawal from Aquidneck Island after the failed siege of Newport. The victory of Sullivan and Greene in this battle, the largest in the history of New England, prevented the capture of a five-thousand-man American army by a British force of comparable size and ensured its safe and unimpeded evacuation to the mainland.

In October 1780, Greene received the military opportunity for which he had worked and studied: command of the southern theatre of war, replacing General Horatio Gates, who had just been routed at the Battle of Camden. When Congress granted Washington the discretion to choose a new commander, he unhesitatingly selected Greene, who accepted the appointment with enthusiasm, having resigned his quartermaster post in disgust in August 1780. En route south, Nathanael stopped at Philadelphia to make a successful request that the troops commanded by Virginia's Henry "Light Horse Harry" Lee be added to his army.

During a campaign of less than two years' duration, Greene justly earned a reputation as "strategist of the Revolution" and proved as adroit at hit-

and-run warfare and strategic retreat as General George Patton would at sustained offense. Greene took command of a depleted force of twenty-two hundred men, two-thirds of whom were militia, at Charlotte, North Carolina, on December 3, 1780. Learning that his foe, Lord Charles Cornwallis, was awaiting reinforcements in Winnsboro, South Carolina, Greene divided his small force before these reinforcements could arrive, sending Daniel Morgan with six hundred riflemen to shadow Cornwallis, while Greene rebuilt his own army. Morgan scored a brilliant victory over the brutal British cavalry leader Banastre Tarleton at Cowpens on January 17, 1781, and a reinforced Greene headed north through the breadth of North Carolina to rendezvous with Morgan across the Dan River into Virginia, a move military historians have described as "masterful."

Acquiring additional troops in Virginia, Greene recrossed the Dan with forty-two hundred soldiers to battle Cornwallis at Guilford Courthouse, North Carolina. On March 15, Greene retreated after a furious fight, but not before inflicting casualties on approximately 30 percent of the British force. Cornwallis headed for the coast at Wilmington to reorganize. Then he made his fateful decision to march north to Yorktown, where his battered army might be evacuated in the event of additional military damage.

While a badly bruised Cornwallis headed north, Greene went south with fifteen hundred Continental troops to engage a total of eight thousand British troops garrisoned throughout South Carolina and Georgia and occupying both Charleston and Savannah. Fortunately, he had the assistance of such able, daring and resourceful "partisans" as Thomas Sumter, Andrew Pickens and "the Swamp Fox" Francis Marion. Often outnumbered, Greene fought skirmishes (rather than large pitched battles) with the British and their Loyalist allies at Hobkirk's Hill, at Fort Ninety Six and at bloody Eutaw Springs, near Charleston. Greene was forced from the field in each encounter during his relentless campaign of attrition, prompting him to utter his famous remark: "We fight, get beat, rise, and fight again."

Aided by General "Mad" Anthony Wayne and "Light Horse" Harry Lee, Greene's constant pressure (akin to guerilla warfare) and his gradual control of the interior areas of Georgia and South Carolina first forced the British to the coast and then induced them to evacuate Charleston and Savannah in 1782. Both towns hailed the Rhode Islander as their liberator.

After the conflict formally ended in 1783, North and South Carolina and Georgia granted Greene money or estates in gratitude for his heroic service. Although he returned to Rhode Island briefly, his huge personal war debts prompted him and Caty to seek a more promising economic future in Georgia, after twice refusing offers from the Confederation Congress to become secretary of war. Of his several land grants, Greene chose the Mulberry Grove plantation, fourteen miles outside Savannah, as his new home. He took up residence there in 1785, but he died of sunstroke on June 19 of the following year at the age of forty-four, before he could extricate himself from debt, leaving Caty and her young children to fend for themselves in a new and challenging environment.

Greene is regarded by military historians as Washington's ablest general. Other than Washington himself and Henry Knox, he was the only general to serve the entire eight years of the war. Thomas Jefferson, the wartime governor of Virginia, asserted that Greene had no equal as a military thinker among his peers in the officer corps. Numerous cities, counties, schools and parks are named for Greene across America, especially in the South. A monument to Greene, under which his remains are interred, stands in Johnson Square, Savannah; his statue, with that of Roger Williams, represents the state of Rhode Island in the National Hall of Statuary in Washington's Capitol Building; his homes in Potowomut and Coventry's village of Anthony are well preserved; and the Rhode Island Historical Society has completed a thirteen-volume critical edition of his papers, published by the University of North Carolina Press. Both his military ardor and his humane spirit are best expressed to our age by Greene himself: "We are soldiers who devote ourselves to arms, not for the invasion of other countries but for the defense of our own; not for the gratification of our private interests but for public security."

Catharine Littlefield Greene

Catharine Littlefield Greene (1755–1814) was the vivacious, free-spirited and uninhibited wife of General Nathanael Greene, but by the standards of her time, she was so much more.

Born on Block Island, the daughter of John Littlefield, a colonial legislator, and Phebe Ray, she moved to Warwick at age ten after the death of her mother. Here she was raised and instructed in the social graces by her aunt and namesake, Catharine Ray, the wife of future governor William Greene Jr. and the sister-in-law of Governor Samuel Ward.

In 1774, nineteen-year-old "Caty" married William Greene's distant cousin, thirty-two-year-old Nathanael Greene, a Quaker by faith and

The Revolutionaries

Unfortunately painted in her old age, the only likeness that exists of Catharine Littlefield Greene does not capture the youthful beauty nor the unconventional individualism of General Greene's popular and vivacious wife or what her biographers have described as her "spirited, cheerful presence at army headquarters during the Revolution." The unsigned portrait hangs in the Telfair Academy of Arts and Sciences in Savannah, Georgia.

an ironmonger by trade. Within a year of their marriage, Nathanael had actively embraced the Revolutionary cause and moved from the ranks of the Kentish Guards, a local militia unit, to the rank of brigadier general in the Continental army.

Caty joined her husband at his camps during the war, a privilege his rank allowed. Most notable was her sojourn during the winter of 1777–78 at Valley Forge, where she won the friendship and admiration of George Washington for her fortitude and high spirits. Described by her biographers, John and Janet Stegeman, as "uninhibited, witty, pretty, a stimulating conversationalist, and raconteur," as well as a voracious reader, she established firm friendships with such Revolutionary leaders as Lafayette, Alexander Hamilton and Generals Henry Knox and "Mad" Anthony Wayne.

The lack of financial opportunity available to the Greenes in New England after the war prompted them to accept grants of land offered by the grateful State of Georgia to its liberator. The most desirable gift was the Mulberry Grove plantation near Savannah, next to an estate owned by General Wayne. In 1786, as this venture was beginning to prosper, Nathanael died suddenly of "sunstroke," leaving Caty and their five children to struggle on.

The Greenes had fortunately brought their children's tutor, Yale graduate Phineas Miller, to Mulberry Grove. He became Caty's helpmate and, eventually, her husband in 1796. Miller also was responsible for the visit of another Yale graduate, Eli Whitney, to Mulberry Grove. By the time of Whitney's arrival, Caty had won her long and courageous battle with the federal government to be reimbursed for the many expenditures made by her late husband in the prosecution of the War for Independence—an award of $47,000, blessed by President Washington. With this money, she invested in several business projects, including the efforts of Whitney to develop a machine for removing (or ginning) the seeds from cotton.

Unfortunately, the cotton gin was not an immediate financial success. This disappointment and other risky investments in land resulted in the sale of Mulberry Grove for back taxes. Caty and Miller then moved to another parcel granted to General Greene on Cumberland Island off the Georgia coast and built a home there that they called Dungeness. When her husband died tragically in 1803 of blood poisoning from a thorn wound, Caty was widowed for a second time. Undaunted, she managed her plantation, continued her business dealings and engaged in social activities at Dungeness, although often burdened with debt. On September 2, 1814, in the midst of another war with England, this unconventional, influential and dynamic woman died of "coastal fever" at the age of fifty-nine.

COLONEL WILLIAM BARTON

William Barton (1748–1831), of Warren and Providence, was a Revolutionary army colonel whose most notable exploit was leading a daring raid in July 1777 to seize General Richard Prescott, the commander of the British forces occupying Aquidneck Island.

Born in the town of Warren, the son of Benjamin and Lydia Barton, William Barton received a common-school education. He then embarked on the trade of hat making, married Rhoda Carver and moved to Providence, where he acquired the lot on which the Industrial Trust/Fleet Bank Building now stands.

In 1775, Barton joined the Rhode Island militia and rose rapidly to the rank of major. Two years later, he developed and carried out a scheme to capture British general Richard Prescott, whose occupation of Newport from December 1776 onward had been characterized by arrogance and harshness. On the evening of July 9, 1777, his small, handpicked force of forty volunteers glided in five whaleboats from Warwick Neck past three

The Revolutionaries

British frigates and landed near the Portsmouth-Middletown line. With the aid of Portsmouth's John Hunt, Barton and his men advanced inland from the western shore of Aquidneck to the Overing House, where Prescott slept, presumably with mistress Overing, the owner of the farm. After subduing the sentries, Barton snatched the partially clothed general and transported him across the bay to Warwick. In accordance with Barton's original plan, Prescott's freedom was later purchased in exchange for the captured American general Charles Lee. The site of the raid, now known as the Prescott Farm, is a major state historical site owned and administered by the Newport Restoration Foundation.

The spectacular foray by Barton even earned the admiration of British officer and diarist Captain Frederick Mackenzie, who observed that the raid was "executed in a masterly manner."

"It is certainly a most extraordinary circumstance," said Mackenzie, "that a General commanding a body of 4,000 men, encamped on an island surrounded by a Squadron of Ships of War, should be carried off from his quarters in the night by a small party of the enemy from without and without a shot being fired." London newspapers had little sympathy for Prescott and printed the following rhyme of ridicule:

> *What various lures there are to ruin man,*
> *Women, the first and foremost, all bewitches,*
> *A nymph thus spoiled a general's mighty plan,*
> *And gave him to the foe without his breeches.*

For his exploit, Barton was promoted to colonel by the Continental Congress. In May 1778, he was seriously wounded near Bristol Ferry while chasing a British and Hessian force, under Lieutenant Colonel John Campbell, that had just raided Warren and Bristol. The injury prevented Barton from engaging in the siege of Newport and the ensuing Battle of Rhode Island (August 29, 1778), but the staging area in Tiverton for the July-August siege was named Fort Barton in his honor. When Barton recovered in 1779, he was appointed commander of a light corps consisting of four companies that had been authorized by the Rhode Island General Assembly. He served actively for the remainder of the war.

From 1788 through 1790, Barton campaigned vigorously for the adoption of the federal Constitution. He was a leading delegate to the abortive March 1790 South Kingstown convention, serving as its "monitor," and in May 1790 he cast one of the four Providence votes for ratification. He was then

Colonel William Barton performed the boldest Revolutionary War exploit by a Rhode Islander on the evening of July 9, 1777, when he seized the overly complacent and half-clad British major general Richard Prescott from a farmhouse in Portsmouth. Rumor persists that the general left the security of Newport for a romantic rendezvous with his hostess. Prescott's freedom was later purchased in an exchange for the captured American general Charles Lee. Barton's unsigned portrait (ca. 1780) shown here is in the possession of the Rhode Island Historical Society.

dispatched to New York to notify President Washington of Rhode Island's belated entrance to the Union.

Later in life, Barton became involved in a dispute over land in Barton, Vermont, a town he helped to found. In a legal contest over ownership, a judgment was assessed against him, which, in principle, he refused to pay. As a result, Barton spent nearly fourteen years confined to the Green Mountain State as a debtor. When the Marquis de Lafayette visited America in 1824–25 for a triumphal tour, he learned of his old ally's financial plight and paid Barton's obligation, thereby securing the aged hero's release. Barton returned in honor to Providence, where he died in 1831.

CAPTAIN STEPHEN OLNEY

Stephen Olney (1756–1832), of North Providence, was one of Rhode Island's most distinguished and longest-serving officers during the War for Independence. He was a fifth-generation descendant of Thomas Olney, a joint proprietor with Roger Williams in the settlement of Providence. In 1774, at the age of eighteen, Stephen Olney became a private in a newly chartered militia company called the North Providence Rangers. From that time through the siege of Yorktown in 1781, he participated heroically in numerous military campaigns, rising to the rank of captain.

Olney's early service was with the Second Rhode Island Regiment, and with this outfit he participated in the Battle of Bunker Hill (1775); the Brooklyn Heights campaign (1776); the Battle of Long Island (1776); the Battle of White Plains (1776); the Battle of Princeton (1777), where Olney saved the life of future U.S. president James Monroe by carrying the wounded Virginian to safety; the defense of Fort Mercer at Red Bank, New Jersey (1777); the Battle of Monmouth (1778); the Battle of Rhode Island (1778); the Battle of Springfield, New Jersey (1780), where he was wounded in the arm by a rifle shot; and the siege of Yorktown (1781).

At Yorktown, the decisive battle of the Revolution, Olney led a company in the division commanded by General Lafayette, a detachment that attacked one of two advanced redoubts of the British. In this heroic charge, Olney received three bayonet wounds, but he soon recuperated. In March 1782, he resigned his commission and returned home because he felt that his gallantry at Yorktown had not been properly acknowledged.

Captain Stephen Olney served from Bunker Hill in June 1775 to Yorktown in October 1781, when he was severely wounded in a heroic charge against British fortifications. Amazingly, he never rose beyond the rank of captain, even though he had a war record more distinguished than nearly all other Rhode Islanders. Olney left no portrait other than a caricature engraving on an 1822 bank note, but his farmhouse, which he erected about 1790 near the site of his birthplace, still stands. His grave is located a short distance from the house and is marked by a plain slate stone on which is recorded a brief history of his military service.

Olney married just prior to the war and had eight children by his first wife, who died in 1813. After the war, he played a prominent role in the political life of North Providence as a longtime member of the General Assembly and as president of the town council. Captain Olney's final years were spent in Johnston, to which he moved in 1826 after his marriage to a widow from that town.

One of his most emotional experiences in later life occurred in 1824, when General Lafayette visited Providence on the Frenchman's triumphal tour of America. Lafayette met Captain Olney, his old comrade in arms, on the steps of the statehouse in Providence, and each embraced the other with such warmth and affection that, according to one observer, "among the many hundreds who witnessed this honest and patriotic effusion of tenderness, scarcely a dry eye was to be seen."

Although Olney served for six years and ten months in the American army, fought in numerous pitched battles and suffered severe wounds in two encounters, his angry resignation after the Yorktown victory excluded him from a Revolutionary War pension program later enacted by Congress that provided relief only to those who served until war's end. Needing money to maintain a decent standard of living, in 1828 Olney petitioned Congress for inclusion in its pension system. Through the efforts of Rhode Island congressmen Dutee Pearce and Tristam Burges, Congress passed "An act for the relief of Stephen Olney" on

May 28, 1830, a measure that made his final years more comfortable financially. However, they were not comfortable physically. He died on November 23, 1832, at the age of seventy-seven from complications arising from the amputation of his arm because of a cancerous growth.

Olney was given a hero's funeral, and the newly established *Providence Journal* eulogized that "he was in the best and highest sense of the words, a Patriot and a Republican, devotedly attached to our national institutions and interests, for which in his younger days, he had so often been ready to make the sacrifice of his life." Olney's home still stands at 138 Smithfield Road, North Providence, and his grave site is nearby.

CAPTAIN SILAS TALBOT

Silas Talbot (1751–1813) was born in Dighton, Massachusetts, into a poor farm family, the son of Benjamin Talbot and Rebecca Allen. His mother died when he was four. In his early teens, Silas worked on a coasting vessel and then learned the stonemason's craft. In 1769 or 1770, he moved to Providence to ply his trade. Talbot prospered in his new home, and in 1772 he married Anna Richmond, who bore him five children before her death in 1781. Two of his children died in infancy.

Talbot became an officer in the Rhode Island militia at the beginning of the Revolution. He was present at the siege of Boston in 1775–76, and he participated in the military campaigns around New York and Philadelphia and was wounded in both. In New York, his injuries stemmed from his attempt to aid Washington's retreat from Long Island. Talbot commanded a fire ship that recklessly rammed the HMS *Asia* in the Hudson River, a daring feat that left him severely burned. He recovered in time to participate in the defenses of Fort Mifflin near Philadelphia, only to be wounded again. After fighting in the Battle of Rhode Island, guarding the Americans' right (west) flank, Talbot embarked on a series of spectacular military and naval exploits.

Ironically, Talbot, an army man, was the only Rhode Island captain of a U.S. naval vessel who maintained an unsullied reputation during the Revolution (Esek Hopkins and Abraham Whipple, for example, drew strong congressional criticism). From 1778 onward, Talbot occasionally got command of a ship, and when he did, sparks flew. In October 1778, in

Of all Rhode Island Revolutionary heroes, except perhaps James Varnum, Captain Silas Talbot enjoyed the most varied and impressive career. He was originally an army man who became captain of a naval vessel in the Revolution. After the War for Independence, he served as a U.S. congressman from New York, captained the USS *Constitution* ("Old Ironsides") and fought in the Quasi-War with France. This artist's sketch was published in Welcome A. Greene's *The Providence Plantations for 250 Years* (1886).

attacking the British schooner *Pigot,* which was blocking the mouth of the Sakonnet River, Talbot plunged the jib boom of his sloop *Hawk* into the *Pigot*'s rigging, holding the British vessel tight while his men overran it. In July 1779, while in command of the *Argo* in defense of the southern New England coast, Talbot captured a ten-gun British privateer and two other vessels of twelve and fourteen guns, recapturing as well the three American ships that the British vessels had in tow. This feat by an army lieutenant colonel prompted Congress in September 1779 to grant him the rank of captain in the Continental navy, but when Congress could give him no ship to command, he became a privateer.

In 1780, while commanding John Brown's privateer *George Washington,* Talbot was captured by the *Culloden,* a much larger seventy-four-gun British ship of the line. Confined first aboard the notorious prison ship *Jersey,* Talbot was eventually sent to Mill Prison in England, from which he was released in 1781 through the efforts of Benjamin Franklin and John Jay after several futile attempts to escape.

In 1786, Talbot left Providence and moved to New York's Mohawk Valley, where he bought the home and part of the lands that had been confiscated from the family of Sir William Johnson, the noted Indian agent. The widower Talbot then married Rebecca Morris, a member of a prominent Philadelphia family, with whom he had two more children before her death in 1803.

In 1792, Talbot was elected to the New York legislature, and in the following year he was chosen a U.S. congressman with Federalist backing. He resigned the congressional office in 1794 in anticipation of his appointment as captain of a proposed U.S. naval frigate and supervised the construction of the USS *President*. In 1798, during the Quasi-War with France, Talbot finally got his naval command—the frigate *Constitution* ("Old Ironsides"), which he took on two cruises in the West Indies. There he captured several French privateers while convoying American merchant ships.

Following this limited naval war, Captain Talbot resigned his commission, left the navy and moved to New York City. In 1808, he entered into a stormy third marriage with Elizabeth Pintard, from whom he separated in the following year. Talbot died in New York City on June 30, 1813, and is buried at Trinity Churchyard. It is said that during his perilous career Talbot was wounded or injured thirteen times and carried five bullets in his body.

JOSEPH BROWN

Joseph Brown (1733–1785), the son of Captain James Brown and Hope Power, was a noted businessman, scientist, professor and architect and one of the famous Brown brothers who dominated civic life in Providence during the second half of the eighteenth century. Although he was a successful merchant and the manager of his family's spermaceti candle works in Fox Point, his heart and mind were also occupied by more learned enterprises, despite a limited education occasioned by his father's death when Joseph was only five.

Brown is best known for his role in making observations of the transit of the planet Venus across the sun's face in 1769, a project on which he collaborated with Benjamin West of Philadelphia and other astronomers around the world. By comparing transit measurements made at different sites, scientists were able to determine the parallax of the sun and, from this, the dimensions of the solar system.

Aside from astronomy, Brown was interested in chemistry, electricity, meteorology and architecture. In 1772, he supervised the assembly of a new fire engine for Providence, and in 1780 he constructed an improved steam engine to pump water out of the iron ore mines in Cranston that supplied his family's Hope Furnace in Scituate. In 1775, Brown helped to erect a high beacon to warn the Greater Providence area of the approach of British vessels, and he supervised the casting and boring of Revolutionary

War cannons at the Hope Furnace. In 1781, he served in the General Assembly as a deputy from Providence.

Between 1770 and 1785, the versatile Brown designed several of Providence's most notable buildings, including University Hall (the "College Ediface"), the First Baptist Meetinghouse, the Market House, his own mansion at 50 South Main Street and his brother John's house on Power Street (the "John Brown House"). The latter structure was described by John Quincy Adams as the "most magnificent and elegant mansion in America."

A trustee of Rhode Island College (soon to bear his family's name) from 1769 until his death, Brown taught students there and conducted experiments for them. In 1784, when the college struggled to resume activities after the war, he volunteered to serve as professor of experimental philosophy without pay. Death—the result of a stroke—cut short his academic career in 1785. At the time of his death, Joseph Brown was an elected member of the American Academy of Arts and Sciences, recognized for his work and his achievements.

Joseph Brown left no likeness, but he left Providence's most notable eighteenth-century buildings as his memorials. The First Baptist Church, of which he was the principal architect and his brother, John, the contractor, was completed in 1775 on North Main Street. Above its vestibule, a wooden steeple rises 185 feet skyward, making it one of America's tallest structures at the time of its completion.

MOSES BROWN

Moses Brown (1738–1836), a prominent Providence merchant, reformer and philanthropist, was one of the five Brown brothers, a group that included John, Joseph, Nicholas and James, the eldest, a twenty-six-year-old ship captain when he died at sea in 1751. They were the children of Captain James Brown and Hope Power, the great-granddaughter of Nicholas Power, an immigrant from Ireland. Only a year old when his father died, Moses received a few years of formal schooling before being adopted and apprenticed to his wealthy uncle Obadiah to learn the intricacies of eighteenth-century trade and commerce. Moses remained an influential businessman well into the nineteenth century.

In 1764, Moses Brown married his cousin Anna, the daughter of his uncle Obadiah. The couple had three children—Sarah, Obadiah and a daughter who died shortly after birth. Anna's death in 1773 had a powerful impact on Moses and influenced his later humanitarian pursuits.

Moses served as a deputy in the General Assembly from 1764 until 1771 and was an influential political ally of Governor Stephen Hopkins. During this period, he also assisted his brother Joseph in several scientific endeavors, worked to relocate Rhode Island College (established 1764) from Warren to Providence and served as supervisor of the pesthouse in Providence, where he advocated inoculation to prevent communicable diseases.

In 1774, after the death of his first wife, Moses converted from his Baptist beliefs to the Quaker religion, a move that greatly influenced his life and career. He vigorously espoused the reform goals of the Quakers, especially abolitionism and opposition to the foreign slave trade. His views on these subjects placed him at odds with his more wealthy and equally influential brother John. Moses strongly supported the Revolutionary effort, and despite the Constitution's compromise with slavery, he became a leading Federalist.

Moses freed his own slaves on terms that were advantageous to them, he advocated Rhode Island's 1774 ban on further importation of slaves, he fought for the passage of the state's gradual manumission act of 1784 and he helped to secure the passage of a statute in 1787 forbidding anyone to outfit slaving voyages in Rhode Island's ports. By 1789, he had reached the conclusion that the Constitution should be ratified because of the economic stability it would bring and because it at least allowed for banning the slave trade after January 1, 1808.

Moses Brown did a disservice to his historical image by waiting until he was in his nineties to have his portrait painted. Perhaps his Quaker beliefs influenced that decision. The real Moses Brown was a dynamic merchant, industrialist, abolitionist, humanitarian, social reformer and community leader. Shown in the style of his Quaker faith, this unsigned portrait of Moses is attributed to Henry Kinney. It is a late nineteenth-century copy of a work by John Wesley Jarvis, reproduced courtesy of the Annmary Brown Memorial Library.

In 1790, Moses Brown was a silent partner in a textile venture with William Almy and Smith Brown that subsidized the plan of English immigrant Samuel Slater to build the first water-powered Arkwright spinning mill in the United States, an event lavishly hailed by some as the beginning of America's Industrial Revolution. Slater's arrival was induced by a December 12, 1789 letter to him from Moses urging him to "come and work our machines, and have the credit as well as the advantage of perfecting the first water mill in America." Via the firm of Brown and Almy, Moses Brown and his associates provided much of the capital that financed the rapid construction of additional textile mills throughout southern New England.

During his final decades, Moses became widely respected for his philanthropy and his educational endeavors. He was determined to provide sectarian schooling for Quakers, and despite early failures he was instrumental in establishing a Friends' school in Providence by 1819. This now venerable educational institution came to bear his name in 1904. Among his many other civic projects were the Rhode Island Bible Society, the Rhode Island Peace Society and the Providence Athenaeum.

In 1779, Moses had married Mary Olney, who died in 1798. A year later, he took a third wife, Phoebe Lockwood, who died in 1808. His only son, Obadiah, named for his grandfather, became a prominent merchant and businessman who partnered with Moses in several successful ventures, including the firm of Brown and Almy. When Obadiah died in 1822, he left

The Revolutionaries

a gift of $100,000 to the Friends' school founded by his father; it was the largest single bequest made to any American institution of learning up to that time.

Born in the reign of George II, Moses Brown lived to receive a visit from President Andrew Jackson and Vice President Martin Van Buren before his death in Providence on September 6, 1836, a week before his ninety-eighth birthday.

REVEREND SAMUEL HOPKINS

Samuel Hopkins (1721–1803) was a Congregational theologian and reformer. He was born in Waterbury, Connecticut, the son of Timothy Hopkins, a successful farmer with the financial means to send young Samuel to Yale, from which he graduated in 1741. During his senior year at Yale, then operating under Congregational auspices, Hopkins became caught up in the religious revivalism that has come to be known as the Great Awakening. He later claimed to have experienced spiritual conversion at that time.

In 1741, he moved to Northampton, Massachusetts, to prepare for the ministry under the tutelage of the famed revivalist Jonathan Edwards. Two years later, Hopkins accepted the pastorate of the congregation at Great Barrington, Massachusetts (then Housatonic), thus beginning a twenty-six-year ministry on the New England frontier. There, in 1748, he married Joanna Ingersoll, with whom he had eight children.

While serving at Great Barrington, Hopkins published two major theological works that made him the leader of an innovative hyper-Calvinist movement within New England Congregationalism, a movement that was referred to as the New Divinity or Hopkinsianism. Its doctrinal positions (e.g., God does not merely permit sin; He wills it into existence for good ends) and its concept of immediate conversion (a tenet that seemed to diminish the importance of the means of grace—namely prayer, Bible reading and church attendance) prompted increasing criticism, especially from Hopkins's own congregation. In addition, Hopkins was a studious, learned minister, not a skilled or inspiring preacher or an effective revivalist. These factors contributed to his dismissal from rural Great Barrington in 1769 and his momentous move to cosmopolitan Newport's First Congregational Church.

129

The Reverend Samuel Hopkins expounded on the American Revolution's themes of liberty and freedom and applied them to African Americans. He claimed that British attacks on American liberty were providential punishment for the oppression of blacks. From his Newport pulpit, this Congregational clergyman urged both the abolition of slavery and what he called "disinterested benevolence." This likeness of Hopkins is from an engraving by H.W. Smith in Hayward and Blanche Cirker's *Dictionary of American Portraits* (1967).

Hopkins labored in this seaport town for thirty-three years until his death in 1803. In Newport, he not only continued to develop the New Divinity and formulated his doctrine of disinterested benevolence, a radical selflessness for the glory of God and the good of humankind, but he also began to see the connection between disinterested benevolence and the antislavery cause. In 1776, he published *A Dialogue Concerning the Slavery of African Americans*, addressed to the Continental Congress, in which he insisted that the Revolutionary cause would not prosper until freedom was extended to slaves. In the *Dialogue* and other pamphlets, Hopkins linked the Revolution and slavery in a framework that became a central element in the first major antislavery movement in America.

While continuing his antislavery crusade, Hopkins also made important contributions to his theology of the New Divinity, especially in a monumental two-volume treatise, published in 1793, entitled *System of Doctrines Contained in Divine Revelation*. According to his biographer Joseph Conforti, "Hopkins was among the most original theologians America has produced." His New Divinity movement came to dominate New England Congregationalism during the first two decades of the nineteenth century; "his doctrine of disinterested benevolence helped inspire the foreign missionary movement in the United States; and his antislavery writings were republished and read by New England abolitionists."

The Revolutionaries

In 1793, his wife Joanna died, and a year later, at the age of seventy-three, he married Elizabeth West. A stroke in 1799 left Hopkins partially paralyzed, but he survived and continued his theological efforts until his death in December 1803.

Reverend James Manning

Reverend James Manning (1738–1791), Baptist clergyman and founding president of Rhode Island College (now Brown University), was born in Elizabeth Township, New Jersey, to parents who were probably of Irish origin. He attended Hopewell Academy, a Baptist grammar school, and the College of New Jersey (now Princeton), a school that operated under Presbyterian auspices. In 1764, after ordination as a Baptist minister, Manning and his wife, Margaret Stiles, moved to Warren, Rhode Island, where he founded a Latin school and a Baptist church. When the region's Baptists decided, after much debate and controversy, to establish a college in Warren, they obtained a charter from the General Assembly in 1764, after more debate and controversy. Shortly thereafter, the fellows of Rhode Island College chose the Reverend James Manning as the school's first president. By 1770, the college's financial problems and the persuasion of Providence civic leaders, especially Stephen Hopkins and the Brown brothers, had led to its relocation, and Manning moved with it to Providence.

As a Calvinist with an evangelical spirit, Manning was more suited to action than to scholarship. However, he taught classical languages, moral philosophy and rhetoric to his students. Under Manning's leadership, his college attracted and accommodated several religious minorities, including Quakers and Jews.

Manning's arrival in Providence caused a temporary schism in the First Baptist Church. When the pastor and some of the congregation of that church withdrew, Manning became the church's pastor, a position he held from 1770 until 1791. Under his leadership, the First Baptist Church introduced congregational singing, expanded the terms of communion to include more Baptists and moved to a more stringent Calvinistic theology.

During his twenty-one-year tenure in Providence, Manning became a prominent civic leader and even served Rhode Island as a delegate to the Confederation Congress in 1786. Although he was a reluctant revolutionary,

Although he was a Baptist who espoused separation of church and state, the Reverend James Manning was also actively involved in the causes of independence and statehood. He allowed University Hall to be used as a barracks and hospital for American and French troops, he served in the Confederation Congress and he played a prominent role in the ratification of the federal Constitution. This engraving of Manning is from Reuben A. Guild, *The Life and Times of James Manning and the Early History of Brown University* (1864).

Manning became a staunch advocate of the federal Constitution, and he was instrumental in securing support for its ratification from Baptists in Rhode Island and Massachusetts, a state he had criticized for compelling Baptists to pay taxes that supported the established Congregational Church.

Joining the Providence Abolition Society in 1789, Manning was one of the earliest New England Baptists to become involved in the abolitionist movement. In April 1791, he resigned as pastor of the First Baptist Church and requested that the college find a new president. He was still serving in the latter capacity when he suffered a fatal stroke and died, childless, in July 1791.

According to his biographers, Manning's greatest significance lies in his contributions to the institutional development of the Baptist denomination. While the college became a focus of Baptist identity, Manning worked to develop his denomination in other ways, and his influence helped reestablish Calvinism as the theological standard among New England Baptists. This Calvinism, says biographer Charles Dunn, "was not a theological straightjacket, but served as a common reference around which disparate New England Baptists could coalesce and from which they could evolve."

John Carter

John Carter (1745–1814) was born in Philadelphia in 1745, the son of Elizabeth Spriggs and John Carter, a naval officer of Irish ancestry killed in battle two months before his son's birth. During the late 1750s, Carter was apprenticed in the print shop of Benjamin Franklin and David Hall. In 1767, Carter moved to Providence, where printer Sarah Goddard took him as a partner in publishing the *Providence Gazette*. Fourteen months later, Goddard withdrew from the enterprise to join her son in Philadelphia, and Carter continued publishing the *Gazette* on his own "at the Sign of Shakespear's Head" at 21 Meeting Street, a home that he built in 1772. The building is now the property of the Providence Junior League.

John Carter, the successor to Sarah Goddard and the counterpart of Solomon Southwick, advanced the Revolutionary cause as editor of the *Providence Gazette*. A former printer's apprentice to Benjamin Franklin, Carter also led the journalistic fight for ratification of the federal Constitution. This portrait of Carter is in the possession of the Rhode Island Historical Society.

Carter molded public opinion in Providence from 1767 until his retirement in 1814. During the two decades of Revolutionary ferment (1764–1783), he was one of the most productive American printers, publishing more than 40 percent of all Rhode Island imprints. He was a fervent advocate of American and individual liberty, and his *Gazette* was a strong supporter of the Revolutionary cause and the ratification of the federal Constitution. Among his many civic involvements, Carter served as Providence postmaster for twenty years (1772–92) and was a leader of the Federalist Party.

For his February 14, 1814 retirement issue, Carter wrote a retrospective of the *Gazette* in which he accurately described the paper as

> *open for the reception of temperate discussion of public affairs; respectful remonstrances to government…and appeals to the people when their independence has been endangered. It has…abounded with original essays on political, literary, moral, and religious subjects; and…has unceasingly disseminated the orthodox political principles of the Washington school.*

In May 1769, Carter married Amey Crawford in an Anglican ceremony. His daughter Ann, one of their twelve children, married businessman-philanthropist Nicholas Brown II; their son, John Carter Brown, was a noted bibliophile who amassed a huge collection of early American imprints that became the nucleus of Brown University's famed John Carter Brown Library.

MAJOR GENERAL JAMES MITCHELL VARNUM

James Mitchell Varnum (1748–1789)—lawyer, Revolutionary War general and judge—was born in Dracut, Massachusetts, the eldest son of affluent farmer Major Samuel Varnum and his second wife, Hannah Mitchell. He attended Harvard for a year, but his involvement in a student protest prompted him to enroll at Rhode Island College (Brown), where he earned his bachelor's degree with honors in 1769 in that school's first graduating class. He followed this success with a master's degree from the same college in 1772.

Varnum briefly returned to Dracut to teach, but he then decided to reside in Rhode Island and pursue the profession of law. After initial misgivings about independence, he strongly espoused the rebel cause. In 1774, he became an officer of the Kentish Guards, and in May 1775, he gained command of the First Rhode Island Regiment. In December 1776, after several military engagements, he attained the Continental army rank of brigadier general, and he served for a year and a half with Washington in New York, New Jersey and Pennsylvania. Having made a recruitment proposal to George Washington in January 1778 that led to the creation of Rhode Island's Black Regiment, Varnum fought in the Battle of Rhode Island with that new unit. Varnum's criticism of Commanding General John Sullivan after the unsuccessful siege of Newport prompted his resignation from service in the Continental army on March 5, 1779, but he was eventually elevated to the rank of major general in the Rhode Island militia.

In 1780, Varnum was elected to Congress, where he served in 1780, 1781 and 1787. He used his terms as congressman to uphold hard money and creditor's rights in financial matters, and he advocated a stronger, highly centralized national government. His national service sparked Varnum's interest in the newly created western territories.

When many businessmen balked at accepting the paper money issued by Rhode Island's Country Party in 1786 to relieve rural debtors, the General Assembly passed a "force act" imposing criminal penalties on anyone who refused this legal tender. This punishment was to be inflicted by a special

General James Mitchell Varnum—a lawyer, congressman and judge, as well as a military leader—was instrumental in the creation of Rhode Island's so-called Black Regiment and in the development of the doctrine of judicial review. Varnum was a strong supporter of the new federal Constitution. His unsigned posthumous portrait, attributed to Ethan Allen Greenwood, is reproduced courtesy of the Varnum House Museum in East Greenwich.

court without the benefit of trial by jury. After Revolutionary War marine hero John Trevett tendered a bill to his Newport butcher John Weeden, and Weeden declined it, the stage was set in 1786 for *Trevett v. Weeden*, the most important case in Rhode Island's judicial history. The case was heard before the highest court in the state, and it concluded when the court refused jurisdiction and dismissed Trevett's complaint.

In the course of the trial, Varnum, one of Weeden's defense attorneys, advanced a learned and eloquent argument urging the court to exercise its hitherto unused power to review legislation and declare the force act unconstitutional for depriving those accused of trial by jury, which Varnum termed "a first, a fundamental, and a most essential principle, in the English constitution" and a "sacred right" transferred from England to America by numerous royal charters, including Rhode Island's basic law of 1663. Although the court did not act on this plea, Varnum's brief was widely disseminated. It was printed and advertised in several issues of the *Pennsylvania Packet* on the eve of the Constitutional Convention of 1787. While the convention was in progress, Varnum expounded his theory of judicial review to George Washington in a letter dated June 18, 1787, and James Madison alluded to the *Trevett v. Weeden* case on July 17, 1787, during the debates on the "judicial negative" of state laws. It was clearly one of the influences on Chief Justice John Marshall when he established the principle of judicial review in the landmark case of *Marbury v. Madison* in 1803.

Having become a director of the Ohio Company in August 1787, the ambitious Varnum left Rhode Island shortly after the trial to seek his fortune in the newly created Ohio Country. There he was appointed a United States territorial judge and assisted in drafting the territory's first code of laws. Although he was of powerful build and a physical culturist, his health failed in the frontier environment after he contracted tuberculosis. On January 10, 1789, Varnum's death at the age of forty cut short his highly promising career. Contributing to the family's prominence, however, his younger brother Joseph, who remained in Massachusetts, became a Democratic-Republican congressman (1795–1811), Speaker of the House of Representatives in the Tenth and Eleventh Congresses, one of the few New England leaders to support "Mr. Madison's War" of 1812 and, finally, a United States senator (1811–17).

Despite the existence of a family cemetery in Dracut and a house in East Greenwich, General Varnum was buried in Marietta, Ohio. His wife, Martha Child of Warren, whom he married in 1770, remained in Rhode Island and survived her husband by forty-eight years. The couple had no children.

Despite Varnum's expatriation, he is amply remembered in Rhode Island. His historic home survives today in East Greenwich as a house museum, and a local Rhode militia group, the Varnum Continentals, was established in 1907 to honor his memory. This unit maintains the Varnum Memorial Armory, erected on Main Street in East Greenwich in 1914, which contains a fine military and naval museum. In addition, the general is memorialized by Camp Varnum in Narragansett, the main educational center of the Rhode Island Army National Guard.

SIGNER AND CONGRESSMAN WILLIAM ELLERY

William Ellery (1727–1820), merchant, congressman, chief justice and signer of the Declaration of Independence, was the son of prominent Newport merchant William Ellery and Elizabeth Almy. His well-to-do father sent him to Harvard, from which young William graduated in 1747. He then embarked on a mercantile career, but when his father's death in 1764 left him with a considerable inheritance, Ellery began to engage actively in politics as an ally of Governor Samuel Ward. He was an early supporter of the protest movement against England and joined the Newport Sons of Liberty in the mid-1760s.

By 1769, Ellery had deemphasized his mercantile activity in favor of a career in law and government, and he was admitted to the bar in 1770. At the death of Samuel Ward, who had been representing Rhode Island in the Continental Congress, Ellery was chosen by the General Assembly to succeed his mentor. He arrived in Philadelphia just in time to join with Stephen Hopkins in signing the Declaration of Independence.

Ellery served in the Continental Congress throughout the Revolution, developing a special interest in naval affairs. In 1779, he was chosen a member of the newly constituted Board of Admiralty. On July 9, 1778, he joined with delegates Henry Marchant and John Collins in signing the Articles of Confederation for Rhode Island, hailing this first national constitution as the "Grand Corner Stone" of the new nation. Ellery was also a Rhode Island delegate to the Confederation Congress until he returned from Philadelphia in 1785 to accept election by the legislature as chief justice of Rhode Island's highest court, a post he held for a one-year term.

Ellery played a major role in Rhode Island's ratification of the federal Constitution and even conspired with such members of the U.S. Congress as Benjamin Huntington of Connecticut and John Adams of Massachusetts to pressure Rhode Island into joining the Union. His efforts on behalf of Federalism were rewarded handsomely when President George Washington appointed him to the lucrative post of collector of customs for Newport, a position Ellery held from 1790 until his death in 1820 at the age of ninety-two, during a time when tariff duties were the principal source of federal revenue.

As a member of the customs service, Ellery vigorously opposed the effort of James DeWolf of Bristol to create a new customs district in that port town and appoint as collector Charles Collins, a slave trader who would turn a blind eye toward DeWolf's illegal involvement in that notorious traffic. Despite Ellery's protest, President Thomas Jefferson sided with the wealthy and influential DeWolf and approved the creation of a separate Bristol district in 1801.

William Ellery, one of Rhode Island's two signers of the Declaration of Independence, also signed the Articles of Confederation, and he might have signed all three founding documents if Rhode Island had not boycotted the Philadelphia Convention. He lived until the ripe age of ninety-two. Ellery's initial occupation of merchant made him a good choice for the lucrative post of Newport's collector of customs. This portrait by Samuel Bell Waugh, after a painting by John Trumbull, is reproduced courtesy of the Rhode Island Historical Society.

Ellery's first wife, Ann Remington, died in 1764, leaving him with six children, and in 1767, Ellery married Abigail Carey, with whom he had ten more children. Among Ellery's grandchildren were Richard Henry Dana, the author of the maritime classic *Two Years Before the Mast*; Edward T. Channing, a noted Harvard professor who wrote a biographical sketch of Ellery; and

The Revolutionaries

Reverend William Ellery Channing, the chief spokesman for New England Unitarianism in the mid-nineteenth century. Ellery's nephew Christopher Ellery served as a Democratic-Republican U.S. senator from Rhode Island from 1801 to 1805 and succeeded William as Newport customs collector from 1820 to 1834. Ellery's career is recounted by William M. Fowler Jr. in a biography entitled *William Ellery: Rhode Island Politico and Lord of Admiralty* (1973). William Ellery Park, at Thames and Popular Streets in Newport, has been named in his honor.

CONGRESSMAN JONATHAN HAZARD

Jonathan Hazard (1744–1825) was born to a Newport Quaker family in 1744. As a young man, he moved to rural Charlestown, became a small farmer and also worked as an itinerant tailor. Passionately involved in the movement for independence, during the Revolution he served for a time as the paymaster of the Rhode Island regiment of the Continental army.

In the mid-1780s, when a postwar depression and the taxing policies of the merchant-controlled state government caused hardship in the rural, agricultural areas of Rhode Island, Hazard emerged as the legislative champion of Rhode Island's agrarian debtors. First elected to the General Assembly in 1776, he gathered about him a forceful group of rural politicians in 1785 to form a protest group, which was styled the "Country Party." This new organization devised an ingenious fiscal program based on the issuance of £100,000 of paper money, an amount about equal to Rhode Island's war debt. According to Hazard's plan, farmers could borrow this money to pay their overdue taxes and other debts, using their land as security, at an interest rate equivalent to the rate the state was paying on its war bonds. If taxes were continued at existing levels, they would be easier to pay because of the increased money in circulation. Hazard predicted that these taxes would be sufficient to retire the state debt at par in seven years, thus lifting the burden of debt service from the backs of farmers, who paid a hefty land tax to support the operations of state government.

Since the paper money was legal tender and could also be used to discharge private debts, merchants and other creditors—fearing the paper's depreciation—opposed Hazard's plan vehemently. Undaunted, Hazard's

This note is from the paper-money issue of 1786, orchestrated by Charlestown representative Jonathan Hazard. During the nationwide economic depression of the early 1780s, Rhode Island farmers groaned under the heavy land tax imposed on them by the merchant-controlled General Assembly. Hazard led a rural taxpayers' revolt, and his ad hoc "Country Party" seized control of state government in 1786 and passed debtor-relief measures such as a £100,000 land bank so that farmers could borrow this money from the state to pay their delinquent real estate taxes. This bill is from the author's collection.

Country Party seized control of the General Assembly in the 1786 annual election, sent Hazard as the state's delegate to the Confederation Congress and implemented the party's paper-money program. Since the adoption of the proposed federal Constitution could disrupt the new fiscal system by banning state issues of paper currency, the Country Party strongly espoused the cause of Anti-Federalism. Hazard, a democratic localist, also feared the loss of state rights to a powerful central government, and as a Quaker he criticized the Constitution for its three concessions to slavery.

"Beau Jonathan" (as he was called because of his fondness for courtly manners and dress) used his great oratorical skills in both the General Assembly and the Confederation Congress to frustrate the supporters of ratification. In 1790, however, when pressure from Congress made ratification inevitable, Hazard modified his opposition to the Constitution in the hope of gaining Federalist support for election to the U.S. Senate. This maneuver backfired, and the eloquent Beau Jonathan became a scapegoat in the bitter contest over the composition of Rhode Island's first congressional delegation. Federalists unleashed their hatred for the domineering Hazard, the apostle of paper money; the Country Party resented his opportunism and blamed him for its failure to block the Constitution; and the powerful Arthur Fenner of Providence successfully moved to displace him as the party's leader. These factors sealed Hazard's political demise.

The Revolutionaries

The deposed leader, clearly the most influential political figure in Confederation-era Rhode Island, continued to represent Charlestown in the General Assembly until 1805, but his dominance was gone. In that year, Hazard departed Rhode Island with his wife, Patience, and their younger children to reside in Verona, a new Quaker settlement in Oneida County, New York. Here, two decades later, the man who dominated Rhode Island politics during one of its most critical periods died unheralded; even the date of his demise is uncertain.

CONGRESSMAN AND JUDGE HENRY MARCHANT

Henry Marchant (1741–1796), of Newport and South Kingstown, was a well-educated intellectual and a protégé of Ezra Stiles. Marchant was born on Martha's Vineyard, the son of Hexford Marchant, a sea captain. His mother, whose maiden name was Butler, died when he was four, shortly after the family moved to Newport. His father's second bride was a daughter of Governor Samuel Ward, a marriage that gave young Henry his entrée into Newport's political life. Marchant attended the University of Pennsylvania (then the College of Philadelphia) from 1756 to 1759 and received a master's degree in 1762. He also read law under the able tutelage of the renowned Judge Edward Trowbridge of Cambridge, Massachusetts, prior to entering public life as a Ward protégé. In 1765, he married Rebecca Cooke.

An ardent Son of Liberty during the Stamp Act protest of 1765, Marchant served as Rhode Island's attorney general from 1771 to 1777. When the Revolution erupted, he left vulnerable Newport for his South County estate. Although he represented Newport in the General Assembly during the 1780s, he maintained a spacious, well-kept farm in South Kingstown until his death.

Marchant became a Rhode Island delegate to the Continental Congress (1777–79) and signed Rhode Island's assent to the Articles of Confederation on July 9, 1778, along with William Ellery and John Collins. During the Confederation era, he entered the General Assembly, where he served from 1784 to 1790 as a vigorous spokesman for the state's commercial interest. In 1786, Marchant was associated with James Mitchell Varnum in trying the landmark case of *Trevett v. Weeden*, in which Varnum developed a theory of judicial review of statutes for their constitutionality.

As a strong supporter of the new federal Constitution, in 1790 Marchant introduced a successful bill for the call of a ratifying convention, at which he played a leading role. His efforts on behalf of Federalism were rewarded

Among all of his local contemporaries, Henry Marchant exemplified the intellectual as politician. He was a well-educated and well-read lawyer and congressman and also a gentleman farmer. A leader in the fight to ratify the Constitution, Marchant was rewarded for his efforts by an appointment as the first federal judge for the District of Rhode Island. His portrait, by Max Rosenthal, is reproduced courtesy of the Rhode Island Historical Society.

when George Washington appointed him Rhode Island's first federal judge, a post he held from July 1790 until his death in August 1796.

In his judicial post, Marchant had an opportunity to implement the theory regarding judicial review that his co-counsel, James Varnum, had expounded in *Trevett v. Weeden*. In the 1792 case of *Champion and Dickason v. Silas Casey*, two successive federal circuit court panels—the first headed by Chief Justice John Jay; the second, by Associate Justice James Wilson—declared a Rhode Island legislative resolution designed to shield debtor Casey from his creditors to be a law impairing the obligation of contracts and therefore contrary to Article I, Section 10 (the Contract Clause), of the Constitution of the United States. As district judge, Marchant was a member of both three-judge tribunals. The circuit court's ruling was the first decision by a court declaring a state law invalid for violating the federal Constitution. In *West v. Barnes* (1791) Marchant was involved in the first case to be appealed from a district court to the U.S. Supreme Court, but only a procedural matter was involved.

In 1792, Marchant received a doctor of laws degree from Yale. The honor was twofold: it was conferred by his old mentor, President Ezra Stiles, and it was awarded at a commencement in which Marchant's son William received his bachelor's degree.

The Revolutionaries

CONGRESSMAN AND JUDGE BENJAMIN BOURNE

Benjamin Bourne (1755–1808), a leading advocate of Rhode Island's ratification of the federal Constitution, was born in Bristol, the son of Shearjashub and Ruth (Bosworth) Church Bourne, the product of two old-line Bristol families. His father served as chief justice of Rhode Island's highest court from 1778 to 1781.

Bourne received a bachelor's degree from Harvard College in 1775, just in time to play a role in the political and military events of the American Revolutionary era. In the year following his graduation, young Benjamin was appointed quartermaster in the regiment of Colonel Christopher Lippitt and saw service in New York along the lower Hudson in 1776.

Returning to civilian life, Bourne married Hope (Child) Diman, the widow of Captain Benjamin Diman, and embarked on the practice of law. He was elected as deputy (state representative) from Bristol in 1780 and later in the year became a member of the powerful Council of War, which directed Rhode Island's military efforts. He soon moved to Providence to advance his law practice, and he won election as a deputy from that town, serving from 1787 to 1790. In this capacity, he became a prime mover in the Federalist campaign to win ratification of the Constitution and bring Rhode Island into the new federal Union.

With Rhode Island boycotting the proceedings, the Philadelphia framers of the Constitution specified that the document should be approved by state ratifying conventions. Rhode Island alone defied these instructions, holding a popular referendum in March 1788. Outraged Federalists boycotted this unauthorized procedure.

As the other twelve states, one by one, convened ratifying conventions, debated and approved the Constitution and entered the new Union, Rhode Island's Federalists became more insistent, especially Henry Marchant and Benjamin Bourne, who led the fight in the state legislature to secure the passage of a convention call. They finally succeeded in January 1790, in part because of the threat by Congress to levy import duties on Rhode Island goods. In November 1789, Bourne and James Manning of Rhode Island College (Brown University) had been delegated by the citizens of Providence to present a petition to Congress urging it to refrain from such coercive pressure until a ratifying convention was authorized by the General Assembly.

Rhode Island's ratifying convention held two sessions, one at South Kingstown in early March 1790, which was inconclusive, and the crucial Newport gathering in late May. Benjamin Bourne served as one of the

Benjamin Bourne, one of the half dozen most influential advocates of ratification of the federal Constitution, was a veteran of the Revolutionary War, a state legislator, Rhode Island's first U.S. congressman, a federal district court judge and the state's first federal circuit judge. Yet among all of the architects of statehood, Bourne is the least known and honored. Even patriotic Bristol, his hometown, ignores his achievements. Bourne was not the subject of a portrait; only his silhouette survives.

four delegates from Providence. His brother, Shearjashub Bourne Jr., and former lieutenant governor William Bradford were the two pro-Constitution delegates allowed to Bristol at this momentous ratifying convention.

At 5:20 p.m. on Saturday, May 29, 1790, with Providence threatening to secede from the state if the Constitution was rejected, Benjamin Bourne, in the phrase of convention secretary Daniel Updike, "moved for the grand question of adopting or rejecting the federal government." Bourne's motion squeaked through by a vote of thirty-four to thirty-two, the closest margin of any state. His eloquence, and that of William Bradford, Theodore Foster and Henry Marchant, during five days of intense debate set the stage for Rhode Island's belated and grudging entrance into the American Union.

Bourne was rewarded for his leadership in the drive toward statehood when the voters elected him as Rhode Island's first United States congressman in August 1790. He served until 1796, when he resigned to replace Federalist leader Henry Marchant, who had died in office, as judge of the federal district court for Rhode Island. Bourne vacated that post in 1801 to accept an appointment from John Adams as chief judge of the U.S. court for the First Circuit—a post that was abolished by the incoming Jefferson administration, ending Bourne's judicial service on July 1, 1802.

Returning to Bristol, Bourne practiced law there until his death on September 17, 1808—the twenty-first anniversary of the signing of the Constitution by its framers. He is buried at Bristol's historic Juniper Hill Cemetery.

SENATOR WILLIAM BRADFORD

William Bradford (1729–1808), born in Plympton, Massachusetts, was the great-great-grandson and namesake of the famous governor of the Plymouth Colony. Bradford studied medicine in Hingham, Massachusetts, and then opened a practice in Warren a few years after that town's transfer from Massachusetts to Rhode Island in 1747. In 1751, he married Mary LeBaron, the daughter of a Plymouth physician. After gaining a reputation for his skill as a surgeon, Bradford moved his practice to Bristol, the county seat, where he soon became active in town government.

Bradford's name first appears in the Bristol town records in 1758 and remains prominent therein for the next fifty years. In 1761, Dr. Bradford was elected a deputy (i.e., representative) from Bristol in the General Assembly, where he became House Speaker for the first of his eighteen nonconsecutive terms in 1765. In 1762, he was chosen for the first time to serve as Bristol's town moderator, without relinquishing his post in the General Assembly.

Bradford's success in politics turned him away from medicine toward the practice of law. From 1767 onward, the public records list him as "Esquire" rather than "Dr." He did not abandon his role as physician entirely, however. In May 1778, he treated Colonel William Barton when the latter was wounded giving chase to British lieutenant colonel John Campbell and his Hessian band after the sack of Warren and Bristol, and during the American Revolution he was chairman of the legislative committee created to examine the qualifications of surgeons and surgeons' mates.

In 1773, Bradford served as a member of Rhode Island's Committee of Correspondence, and in 1775, he was chosen deputy governor by the General Assembly when Nicholas Cooke moved up to replace deposed Loyalist governor Joseph Wanton. Active in numerous civil and military capacities during the Revolution, Bradford most notably arranged a cease-fire in October 1775 when Captain James Wallace of the HMS *Rose* bombarded Bristol. Bradford performed this service only five days after the death of Mary, his first and only wife.

Bradford was a member of the Rhode Island Committee of Safety and the powerful Council of War, and he served on several committees to coordinate the war effort with neighboring states. In 1780, he chaired a convention of the New England states in Hartford, called for the purpose of furnishing supplies to our French allies. He was elected a Rhode Island delegate to

Senator William Bradford was easily the most influential Bristolian of the late eighteenth century. His home on Metacom Avenue (shown here) was confiscated from the aptly named Loyalist Isaac Royall. Contemporary Bristolians insist on referring to his former residence as "the Governor Bradford House," thereby confusing him with his illustrious ancestor Governor William Bradford of Plymouth Colony and ignoring the fact that the senator's deputy governorship pales in significance to his position as president pro tem of the United States Senate. The image on the Internet and at the Library of Congress that purports to be the senator is actually that of William Bradford of Pennsylvania, the second attorney general of the United States.

the Second Continental Congress in 1776, but the British threat to Rhode Island prompted him to stay home where he was most needed.

In 1777, Deputy Governor Bradford was appointed to lease the estates of Loyalists whose property had been confiscated. In 1783, he purchased one of these estates himself—the home of Bristol's Isaac Royall, built in 1745 and now known as Mount Hope Farm.

Bradford continued to represent Bristol in the General Assembly during the 1780s, but from 1786 to 1790 he was relegated to minority status when the Anti-Federal Country Party seized the reins of state government. His strenuous effort to persuade the legislature to participate in the framing and adoption of the federal Constitution met with little success, until he was able to cast his vote in favor of ratification on May 29, 1790, as one of Bristol's two convention delegates.

Bradford's influential support of the ratification of the Constitution and his long years of public service to his town and state were crowned by his election to the office of United States senator in 1792, replacing Anti-Federal leader Joseph Stanton Jr. of Charlestown. From July 6, 1797, until his resignation from the Senate in October 1797, Bradford held the prestigious post of the Senate's president pro tem.

During his congressional tenure, Bradford surely met often with President Washington in Philadelphia as one of twenty or so Federalist senators. It was apparently one of those meetings that gave rise to the distorted reminiscence by Bradford's daughter of their weeklong encounter with Washington at Mount Hope Farm. Washington in fact never slept there, local legend to the contrary.

Senator Bradford represented Bristol in the Rhode Island General Assembly during the last decade of his eventful life, once again holding the office of Speaker. He died on July 6, 1808, at the age of seventy-eight. Bradford was originally buried at Bristol's East Burying Ground, but his grave was later moved to the family plot in Juniper Hill Cemetery near the resting place of Benjamin Bourne. His meticulously preserved house and farm on Metacom Avenue in Bristol perpetuates his memory.

SENATOR THEODORE FOSTER

Theodore Foster (1752–1828) was born in Brookfield, Massachusetts, in 1752, the son of Judge Jedediah Foster and Dorothy Dwight of Dedham, a descendant of William Pynchon, an original incorporator of the Massachusetts Bay Company and a founder of Springfield, Massachusetts. As a young man, Foster came to Providence to study at Rhode Island College (now Brown University) and graduated in 1770. In 1771, this socially prominent young man married the equally prominent Lydia Fenner, the sister of Arthur Fenner Jr., who would serve as governor of Rhode Island from 1790 to 1806.

Making law and politics his allied professions, Foster was Providence's town clerk from 1775 to 1787 and a deputy from Providence in the General Assembly from 1776 to 1781. In the assembly, he became a close ally of Stephen Hopkins and was appointed secretary of the Rhode Island Council of War. In 1781, the western portion of the town of Scituate was set off as a separate fifty-two-square-mile municipality and named in Foster's honor—an amazing recognition for a twenty-nine-year-old Massachusetts native.

Foster's achievements increased in the years following American independence. In 1785, he was appointed judge of Rhode Island's court of admiralty, and he became a leader in the movement to ratify the federal Constitution. Although the Anti-Federalists rejected him for the post of secretary of the South Kingstown ratifying convention in March 1790, Foster kept valuable and revealing minutes of that body, which were finally edited and published in 1929 by Professor Robert C. Cotner.

Foster's services in support of the Constitution earned him election by the General Assembly as one of Rhode Island's first two United States senators. He began his service on June 7, 1790, with Anti-Federal leader General Joseph Stanton Jr. of Charlestown, his counterpart, joining him in the Senate soon thereafter. Foster served as an ardent Federalist until his retirement in March 1803. For his final three

Theodore Foster, an active Federalist leader, joined with Joseph Stanton Jr., an Anti-Federalist stalwart, to represent Rhode Island in the First Congress. Foster, the brother-in-law of Governor Arthur Fenner, served from June 7, 1790, until March 3, 1803. Upon his retirement, he settled in rural Foster, a town that had been named for him at its creation in 1781 when he was the Providence town clerk. Foster's anonymous portrait is reproduced courtesy of the Rhode Island Historical Society.

years in the upper chamber, he was joined by his brother, Dwight, the U.S. senator from Massachusetts. Like James Mitchell Varnum, Foster was a Massachusetts native whose brother represented the Bay State in each house of Congress: Dwight Foster, a Brown graduate, was a U.S. congressman from March 1793 to June 1800 and a senator from June 1800 to March 1803, when both brothers retired from congressional service.

Theodore Foster was noted not only as a lawyer and a statesman but also as a scholar. He received master's degrees from both Brown (1773) and Dartmouth (1787) and served as trustee of Brown from 1794 until 1822.

The Revolutionaries

Upon his retirement in 1803, he began a life of scholarship on his estate in Foster in concert with a scholarly next-door neighbor, Dr. Solomon Drowne, his classmate at Brown and a prominent botanist and physician who dubbed his estate Mt. Hygeia after the Greek goddess of health. Foster collected numerous documents and letters during his lifetime pertaining to Rhode Island politics. He intended to use these materials (many of which came from Stephen Hopkins) to write a general history of the state. Although that goal was not accomplished, his heirs sold the Foster Papers to the Rhode Island Historical Society, where they constitute a treasure-trove for researchers of the critical era in which Foster played such a central role.

Foster's wife Lydia, who bore him three children, died in 1801, and in 1803, he wed Esther Brown Millard, by whom he had five more children. Foster's last public service was as the representative from Foster to the General Assembly from 1812 to 1816. He died in Providence in 1828 at the age of seventy-five and was interred in Swan Point Cemetery.

CAPTAIN ROBERT GRAY

On August 10, 1790, a week before George Washington completed his trip from New York City to Rhode Island to acknowledge and celebrate the reluctant thirteenth state's entrance to the Union, Captain Robert Gray of Tiverton completed another journey in Boston Harbor: he was the first American to circumnavigate the world.

Gray—who has remained relatively obscure, especially in Rhode Island—was born on a farm in Tiverton on May 10, 1755, to parents who were descended from early Plymouth Colony settlers. His homestead still stands at 3622 West Main Road. It is marked by a small sign donated by the class of 1971 of the Gray Junior High School of Tacoma, Washington.

The seventh of nine children, Gray probably gained his maritime skill by privateering during the American Revolution or by service in the Continental navy, but little is known of his early years. The fact that Boston merchant-investors designated Gray as second in command of a two-ship excursion around Cape Horn to the north Pacific in 1787 is an indication of his experience as a mariner. On this, the first of his two trips to the Great Northwest, Gray commanded the sloop *Washington*, the smaller consort to the ship *Columbia*, commanded by Captain John Kendrick. The primary

Tiverton mariner Robert Gray was the first American to captain a ship that circumnavigated the globe, and he then did it again. Gray's exploration of the Pacific Northwest is comparable to Henry Hudson's voyage in the *Half-Moon* up the river that bears his name, but Gray named his river for his ship, the *Columbia*. Although both Gray and the *Columbia* are well recognized in Washington and Oregon, Captain Gray and his exploits are only dim memories in his native Rhode Island. The unsigned portrait of Gray is reproduced courtesy of the Oregon Historical Society.

purpose of this venture was economic: to acquire furs and sea otter skins for trade with China.

On August 12, 1788, Gray and his crew accomplished the first landing by United States citizens on the Northwest Coast, coming ashore near Cape Lookout in what would become the state of Oregon. This feat was but one of a series of firsts that would be registered by the intrepid Rhode Island sailor.

One must use caution in recording "firsts." During the second half of the eighteenth century, Spain, Great Britain and Russia also developed and asserted claims to the area of the Northwest now designated as the states of Oregon, Washington and Idaho. Several Spanish navigators, a Frenchman and a few British mariners and traders, including the famous Pacific explorer James Cook, beat Gray to this region—hence the use of the specific term "United States citizens" in describing the accomplishment of Gray and his men.

After Gray charted the coastline and secured a shipload of pelts, Captain Kendrick gave him command of the *Columbia* and dispatched him to Macao and Canton, China, via the Sandwich (i.e., Hawaiian) Islands. Following a profitable visit, Gray left Canton on February 12, 1790, with a cargo of silk, porcelain and tea and sailed through the Indian Ocean, around the Cape of Good Hope and north to Boston, arriving on August 10, 1790, thus completing the first American circumnavigation of the globe.

Gray immediately returned to the Northwest aboard the *Columbia*, leaving Boston on September 27, 1790, with a letter of introduction signed by President George Washington and Secretary of State Thomas Jefferson. On this second expedition, Gray achieved yet another distinction: on May 11, 1792, with all sails set to a favorable wind, he boldly raced his ship *Columbia* through coastal breakers, over a perilous sandbar and into a broad river that he named for his vessel. Gray had "discovered" (to use the white man's term) the legendary Great River of the West. The Columbia—"a noble river," as Gray described it—extended inland some 1,243 miles, and its vast watershed drained the Oregon Country.

Gray's expedition established the first substantial American claim to the Pacific Northwest, a claim strengthened and reaffirmed by Lewis and Clark in 1805 and then by fur trader John Jacob Astor in 1811. After his "discovery" of the Columbia River, Gray sailed his previous route to China and thence to Boston, accomplishing the second American circumnavigation of the world. John Boit Jr., an officer and log keeper on *Columbia*'s 1790 journey to Oregon, put Captain Gray's efforts in perspective: "On her first voyage the *Columbia* had solved the riddle of the China trade. On her second, empire followed in the wake."

In 1794, Gray married Martha Atkins in Boston, a union that produced five children—a son who died in infancy and four daughters. During the 1790s, Gray engaged mainly in the coasting trade between Boston and Charleston, South Carolina, but wanderlust again affected him, and in 1798 he set out from Salem in command of the bark *Alert* on another trading voyage around the Horn to the Great Northwest. By that date, a limited, or quasi, naval war had developed with France, and Gray's ship was taken by a French privateer in the South Atlantic and sold in Montevideo, Uruguay. When Gray returned to Massachusetts, he obtained the captaincy of his own privateer, the twelve-gun *Lucy*, and set out to avenge his loss of the *Alert*. In October 1800, however, President John Adams brought the Quasi-War to an end.

After the conflict with France, Gray sailed to England and Brazil before embarking on an ill-fated trip to Charleston in 1806. He died en route, probably of yellow fever, and was buried in the sea that had been his life.

The great English poet Thomas Gray (no relation to Robert) has observed that "the paths of glory lead but to the grave." Since 1806, Robert Gray has lain in a watery grave because a sudden illness terminated his eventful life at the age of fifty-one. Unfortunately, this great Rhode Island navigator experienced no "path of glory." Many American history texts omit him, and most of his fellow Rhode Islanders are oblivious to his existence. The *Columbia*'s intrepid Captain Robert Gray—a gem of the oceans—deserves a better fate.

Suggested Reading and Reference

G eneral books relating to early Rhode Island that place our pioneers in their proper setting and milieu include Sydney V. James, *Colonial Rhode Island: A History* (New York: Scribner, 1975) and *The Colonial Metamorphosis of Rhode Island* (Hanover, NH: University of New England Press, 2000); Patrick T. Conley, *Democracy in Decline: Rhode Island's Constitutional Development* (Providence: Rhode Island Historical Society, 1977); William G. McLoughlin, *Rhode Island: A Bicentennial History* (New York: W.W. Norton, 1978); Irving B. Richman, *Rhode Island: Its Making and Its Meaning, 1636–1683* (New York: G.P. Putnam's Sons, 1908; 2nd ed.); and William B. Weeden, *Early Rhode Island: A Social History of the People* (New York: Grafton Press, 1910). Samuel Greene Arnold's *History of Rhode Island and Providence Plantations* (Providence, RI: 1859–60; 2 vols.), though dated, is the most detailed account of seventeenth- and eighteenth-century Rhode Island. The older, general, multivolume histories of the state by Edward Field, Thomas Williams Bicknell and Charles Carroll contain much information on early Rhode Island, but they are better for reference than for relaxed reading.

On seventeenth-century Aquidneck, see Carl Bridenbaugh, *Fat Mutton and Liberty of Conscience: Society in Rhode Island, 1636–1690* (Providence, RI: Brown University Press, 1974). Carl R. Woodward's *Plantation in Yankeeland: The Story of Cocumscussoc, Mirror of Colonial Rhode Island* (Chester, CT: Pequot Press, 1971) is excellent for describing South County's economic and social life.

Gertrude S. Kimball's *Providence in Colonial Times* (Boston: Houghton Mifflin, 1912) and William R. Staples's *Annals of the Town of Providence* (Providence, RI: printed by Knowles and Vose, 1843) do the same for Providence, but in an antiquarian fashion. The neglected role of women is addressed by Barbara Mills in *Providence, 1630–1800: Women Are Part of Its History* (Bowie, MD: Heritage Books, 2002).

The best general studies of the Revolutionary era are David S. Lovejoy, *Rhode Island Politics and the American Revolution, 1760–1776* (Providence, RI: Brown University Press, 1958); Florence Parker Simister, *The Fire's Center: Rhode Island in the Revolutionary Era, 1763–1790* (Providence: Rhode Island Bicentennial Foundation, 1979); Anthony Walker, *So Few the Brave: Rhode Island Continentals, 1775–1783* (Newport, RI: Seafield Press, 1981); Irwin H. Polishook, *Rhode Island and the Union, 1774–1795* (Evanston, OH: Northwestern University Press, 1969); Patrick T. Conley, *First in War, Last in Peace: Rhode Island and the Constitution, 1786–1790* (Providence: Rhode Island Bicentennial Foundation and Rhode Island Publications Society, 1987); and Frank Greene Bates, *Rhode Island and the Union* (New York: Macmillan Co., 1898).

Of the fifty-six pioneers profiled herein, Roger Williams has attracted, by far, the greatest attention from biographers. The best studies of his life are Samuel H. Brockunier, *The Irrepressible Democrat: Roger Williams* (New York: The Ronald Press Company, 1940), though Williams was not a Democrat in politics; Ola Elizabeth Winslow, *Master Roger Williams* (New York: Macmillan, 1957); and John Garrett, *Roger Williams: Witness beyond Christendom* (New York: Macmillan, 1970). The best studies of Williams's thought are Perry Miller, *Roger Williams: His Contribution to the American Tradition* (Indianapolis, IN: Bobbs-Merrill Co., 1953), though it understates his influence on the First Amendment; Edmund S. Morgan, *Roger Williams: The Church and the State* (New York: Atheneum, 1962); Edwin S. Gaustad, *Roger Williams* (New York: Oxford University Press, 2005); and *Liberty of Conscience: Roger Williams in America* (Grand Rapids, MI: W.B. Eerdmans Pub. Co., 1991).

Many of the men and women profiled herein await their biographer; others need a modern biography. Those who have been studied in book-length works detailing their lives are listed below in the order of their appearance in this book.

Our earliest pioneers are considered in Lawrence C. Wroth, *The Voyages of Giovanni da Verrazzano* (New Haven, CT: Yale University Press, 1970); Alvin G. Weeks, *Massasoit of the Wampanoags* (Scituate, MA: Digital Scanning Corp., 1920); Louise Lind, *William Blackstone: Sage of the Wilderness* (Bowie, MD:

Heritage Books, 1993); Winifred K. Rugg, *Unafraid: A Life of Anne Hutchinson* (Boston: Houghton Mifflin, 1930); Francis J. Bremer, ed., *Anne Hutchinson, Troubler of the Puritan Zion* (Huntington, NY: Robert E. Krieger, 1980); Amy Schrager Lang, *Prophetic Woman: Anne Hutchinson and the Problem of Dissent in the Literature of New England* (Berkeley: University of California Press, 1987); William Dunlea, *Anne Hutchinson and the Puritans: An Early American Tragedy* (Pittsburgh, PA: Dorrance Pub., 1993); Eve LaPlante, *American Jezebel: The Uncommon Life of Anne Hutchinson, the Woman Who Defied the Puritans* (San Francisco: Harper, 2004); Michael P. Winship, *The Times and Trials of Anne Hutchinson: Puritans Divided* (Lawrence: University Press of Kansas, 2005); Henry E. Turner, *William Coddington in Rhode Island Colonial Affairs: An Historical Inquiry* (Providence, RI: S.S. Rider, 1878); Thomas Williams Bicknell, *Story of Dr. John Clarke* (Providence, RI: self-published, 1915); Louis Franklin Asher, *John Clarke, 1609–1676* (Pittsburgh, PA: Dorrance Pub., 1997); Sydney V. James, *John Clarke and His Legacies* (University Park: Pennsylvania State University Press, 1999); Adelos Gorton, *The Life and Times of Samuel Gorton* (Philadelphia: G.S. Ferguson Co. Printers, 1907); Bradford F. Swan, *Gregory Dexter of London and New England, 1610–1700* (Rochester, NY: Printing House of Leo Hart, 1949); and Ruth Plympton, *Mary Dyer: Biography of a Rebel Quaker* (Boston: Branden Pub., 1994).

Joseph Roman's *King Philip: Wampanoag Rebel* (New York: Chelsea House Publishers, 1992) is the only biography of Philip, but there are numerous accounts of King Philip's War, the best of which are Douglas E. Leach, *Flintlock and Tomahawk: New England in King Philip's War* (New York: Norton, 1966); Jill Lepore, *The Name of War: King Philip's War and the Origins of American Identity* (New York: Knopf, 1998); and James D. Drake, *King Philip's War: Civil War in New England, 1675–1676* (Amherst: University of Massachusetts Press, 1999).

Early eighteenth-century Rhode Island is a historical wasteland, inspiring few books. The only biographies of note pertaining to our subjects from this era are John Daniel Wild, *George Berkeley: A Study of His Life and Philosophy* (New York: Russell & Russell, 1962); Romeo Elton, "Memoir of the Reverend John Callender, M.A.," *Collections of the Rhode Island Historical Society* 6 (1838), a long biographical sketch that prefaces Elton's edited reprint of Callender's *Historical Discourse*; and Carl Bridenbaugh, *Peter Harrison: The First American Architect* (New York: Van Rees, 1949).

Despite the remarkable exploits of those herein profiled, the Revolutionary era (1763–1790) in Rhode Island has not yielded many biographical accounts, except for those relating to the life and career of Nathanael

Greene. The reader is directed to the following accounts: Carl Bridenbaugh, *Silas Downer: Forgotten Patriot: His Life and Writings* (Providence: Rhode Island Bicentennial Foundation, 1974); Edmund S. Morgan, *The Gentle Puritan: A Life of Ezra Stiles, 1727–1795* (New Haven, CT: Yale University Press, 1962); Bernhard Knollenberg, ed., *Correspondence of Governor Samuel Ward, March 1775–March 1776, and Genealogy of the Ward Family*, compiled by Clifford P. Monahon (Providence: Rhode Island Historical Society, 1952), a book that contains a lengthy biographical essay; William E. Foster, *Stephen Hopkins: A Rhode Island Statesman* (Providence, RI: S.S. Rider, 1884); Paul R. Campbell, ed., *Stephen Hopkins: The Rights of Colonies Examined* (Providence: Rhode Island Bicentennial Foundation, 1974); Michael Moses, *Master Craftsmen of Newport: The Townsends and the Goddards* (Tenafly, NJ: MMI Americana Press, 1984); John A. McManemin, *Abraham Whipple, Commander of the Continental Navy* (Spring Lake, NJ: Ho-Ho-Kus Pub. Co., 1999); and Charles H. Miller, *Admiral Number One: Some Incidents in the Life of Esek Hopkins, 1718–1802* (New York: William-Frederick Press, 1962).

On General Nathanael Greene, see Theodore Thayer, *Nathanael Greene: Strategist of the American Revolution* (New York: Twayne Publishers, 1960); George Washington Greene, *The Life of Nathanael Greene, Major General in the Army of the Revolution*, 3 vols. (New York: Hurd and Houghton, 1867–1871); Francis Vinton Greene, *Life of Nathanael Greene* (New York: D. Appleton, 1893); Lee P. Anderson and Lisa Skrowronski, *Forgotten Patriot: The Life and Times of Major General Nathanael Greene* (Parkland, FL: Universal Publishers, 2002); Terry Golway, *Washington's General: Nathanael Greene and the Triumph of the American Revolution* (New York: H. Holt, 2005); and Gerald M. Carbone, *Nathanael Greene* (New York: Palgrave Macmillan, 2008).

For the other Revolutionaries, see John F. Stegeman and Janet A. Stegeman, *Caty: A Biography of Catharine Littlefield Greene* (Athens: University of Georgia Press, 1977); Catherine R. Williams, *Biography of Revolutionary Heroes; Containing the Life of Brigadier General William Barton, and also, of Captain Stephen Olney* (Providence, RI: self-published, 1839); Frank H. Swan, *General William Barton* (Providence, RI: Roger Williams Press, 1947); H.T. Tuckerman, *Life of Silas Talbot* (New York: J.C. Riker, 1850); William M. Fowler Jr., *Silas Talbot: Captain of Old Ironsides* (Mystic, CT: Mystic Seaport Museum, 1995); Charles Rappleye, *Sons of Providence: The Brown Brothers, the Slave Trade, and the American Revolution* (New York: Simon & Schuster, 2006); James B. Hedges, *The Browns of Providence Plantations: Colonial Years* (Providence, RI: Brown University Press, 1968); Mack Thompson, *Moses Brown: Reluctant Reformer* (Chapel Hill: University of North Carolina Press, 1962); Joseph A. Conforti, *Samuel*

Hopkins and the New Divinity (Grand Rapids, MI: Christian University Press, 1981); Reuben Aldridge Guild, *The Life and Times of James Manning and the Early History of Brown University* (Boston: Gould and Lincoln, 1864); James M. Varnum, *A Sketch of the Life and Public Services of James Mitchell Varnum* (Boston: D. Clapp and Son, 1906); Donald A. D'Amato, *General James Mitchell Varnum (1748–1789): The Man and His Mansion* (East Greenwich, RI: Varnum House Museum, 1996); Edward T. Channing, *Life of William Ellery* (Boston: Hilliard, Gray, 1836); William M. Fowler Jr., *William Ellery: A Rhode Island Politico and Lord of Admiralty* (Metuchen, NJ: Scarecrow Press, 1973); J. Richard Nokes, *Columbia's River: The Voyages of Robert Gray, 1787–1793* (Tacoma: Washington State Historical Society, 1991); and Francis E. Cross and Charles M. Parkin Jr., *Captain Gray in the Pacific Northwest, 1787–1793* (Bend, OR: Maverick Publications, 1987).

Other biographical information can be gleaned from such standard multivolume reference works as the *Dictionary of American Biography*, the *American National Biography* and the older *Appleton's Cyclopedia of American Biography*. Rhode Island directories include *Representative Men and Old Families of Rhode Island* (Chicago: J.H. Beers & Co., 1908; 3 vols.); *Biographical Cyclopedia of Representative Men of Rhode Island* (Providence, RI: National Biographical Publishing Co., 1881); and Ralph S. Mohr, *Rhode Island Governors for Three Hundred Years* (Providence, RI: Oxford Press, 1959). Also informative is a biographical anthology entitled *Early Religious Leaders of Newport* (Newport, RI: Newport Historical Society, 1917), containing lengthy essays on John Clarke, George Berkeley, Samuel Hopkins and Ezra Stiles. John Williams Haley's *The Old Stone Bank History of Rhode Island* (Providence, RI: Providence Institution for Savings, 1929–44, 4 vols.) contains numerous vignettes and profiles of early Rhode Islanders.

About the Author

Dr. Patrick T. Conley holds an AB from Providence College, an MA and PhD from the University of Notre Dame with highest honors and a JD from Suffolk University Law School. He has published eighteen books, including *Catholicism in Rhode Island: The Formative Era* (1976); *Democracy in Decline: Rhode Island's Constitutional Development, 1775–1841* (1977); *An Album of Rhode Island History, 1636–1986* (1986); *The Constitution and the States* (1988); *The Bill of Rights and the States* (1992), with John Kaminski; *Liberty and Justice: A History of Law and Lawyers in Rhode Island, 1636–1998* (1998); and *The Rhode Island Constitution: A Reference Guide* (2007), with Justice Robert G. Flanders, as well as more than a score of scholarly articles on history, law, ethnic studies, religion and political science.

The youngest person ever to attain the rank of full professor at Providence College, Dr. Conley also practices law and manages a real estate development business. He has served as chairman of the Rhode Island Bicentennial Commission, chairman and founder of the Providence Heritage Commission, chairman and founder of the Rhode Island Publications Society and general editor of the Rhode Island

Ethnic Heritage Pamphlet Series. In 1977, he founded the Rhode Island Heritage Commission. Dr. Conley was also chairman of the Rhode Island Bicentennial (of the Constitution) Foundation and chairman of the U.S. Constitution Council. In May 1995, he was inducted into the Rhode Island Heritage Hall of Fame—one of a handful of living Rhode Islanders who have been accorded that honor.

Presently, he is president of the Rhode Island Heritage Hall of Fame, president of the Heritage Harbor Museum and chairman of the Rhode Island Senior Olympics.

Pat, who is the father of six children and the grandfather of seven, lives in Bristol, Rhode Island, with his wife, Gail, and their dog, Bridget.

www.ingramcontent.com/pod-product-compliance
Lightning Source LLC
Chambersburg PA
CBHW060804100426

42813CB00004B/939